The Names of the Games

The Stories Behind
the Nicknames of 102
Pro Football, Basketball,
Baseball, and Hockey
Teams

MIKE LESSITER

CONTEMPORARY
BOOKS

CHICAGO · NEW YORK

D1053893

Library of Congress Cataloging-in-Publication Data

Lessiter, Mike.
    The names of the games : the stories behind the nicknames of 102
pro football, basketball, baseball, and hockey teams / Michael Lessiter.
      p.   cm.
    Updated ed. of: Name that team! c1987.
    ISBN 0-8092-4477-2 (pbk.) : $4.95
    1. Athletic clubs—United States—Names—History.   2. Athletic
clubs—United States—Directories.   I. Lessiter, Mike.   Name that
team!   II. Title.
GV583.L474   1988
796'.06073—dc19   88-17699
                                                      CIP

Published by Contemporary Books, Inc.
180 North Michigan Avenue, Chicago, Illinois 60601
Manufactured in the United States of America
International Standard Book Number: 0-8092-4477-2

Published simultaneously in Canada by Beaverbooks, Ltd.
195 Allstate Parkway, Valleywood Business Park
Markham, Ontario L3R 4T8 Canada

Illustrations: Greg Kot
Editorial Advisor: Elyce Moschella

*This book is dedicated
with fond memories to my
Grandmother
Donalda Lessiter.*

*Her many talents, high
spirits, fighting attitude,
and love for literature
are an inspiration to
our family to make
the most of what
God has given to us.*

—Mike Lessiter

CONTENTS

MAJOR LEAGUE BASEBALL®

American League
Major League Baseball

Baltimore Orioles

Baltimore Orioles
Memorial Stadium
Baltimore, MD 21218

Team Colors: Orange, Black, and White
Year Founded: 1901—Milwaukee Brewers
Stadium: Memorial Stadium
Seating Capacity: 53,208

THE ORIGINAL BALTIMORE ORIOLES were charter members of the American League in 1901—its inaugural season in pro baseball. The team had been formed in the late 1800s and the team was known as the Lord Baltimores. It was named after George Calvert, the first Lord Baltimore who governed the British colony of Maryland in 1632.

The name was later shortened to the Baltimore Orioles, in recognition of the official state bird of Maryland.

However, after two seasons the club moved to New York, where they became part of the Yankees.

The current Oriole franchise originated in Milwaukee in 1901. After only one season, the team moved to St. Louis where it was renamed the St. Louis Browns.

The Browns were perhaps the most unsuccessful team in Major League history. During the club's 52 seasons, (1902-1953) the club's record was 3,416 wins against 4,465 losses.

In 1953, a group of Baltimore businessmen bought out the Browns and brought the team back to Baltimore which had been without baseball for 51 years. The team was renamed the Orioles, after the original team from the city.

Boston Red Sox

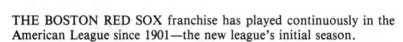

Boston Red Sox
24 Yawkey Way
Boston, MA 02215

Team Colors: Navy Blue, Red, and White
Year Founded: 1901—Boston Americans
Stadium: Fenway Park
Seating Capacity: 33,536

THE BOSTON RED SOX franchise has played continuously in the American League since 1901—the new league's initial season.

Upon entering the American League in 1901, the team was known as the Boston Americans. During the next six years, the names of Pilgrims and Somersets would also be associated with the team.

Although the Boston Red Sox did not become the official name of the team until 1907 under team owner John I. Taylor, it was first used in 1904. The son of the team owner is credited with first calling the team Red Sox because he liked the color of the stockings the Boston players were wearing.

Naming a team after its owner seems to have slowed down. The Detroit Pistons were originally the Fort Wayne Zollner Pistons, named after auto parts manufacturer owner Fred Zollner. Their name worked out well when they moved to the auto city.

Paul Brown, original coach of the Cleveland Browns, was the last man to name a team after himself.

California Angels

California Angels
P. O. Box 2000
Anaheim, CA 92803-2000

Team Colors: Blue, Red, and Gold
Year Founded: 1960
Stadium: Anaheim Stadium
Seating Capacity: 67,335

WHEN FAMOUS COWBOY GENE AUTRY was granted a Major League baseball franchise in 1960, he returned to California without a place to play.

After much work, Autry worked out a deal for the club to play at Los Angeles' Wrigley Field the first season. Now, Autry only needed to find a team name to get settled for the 1961 season.

He chose California Angels for two reasons. First, it was thought Angels was chosen out of respect for the Los Angeles Angels, who played in the Pacific Coast League from 1919-1957. Secondly, the team would be playing in Los Angeles, which is known as the "City of Angels."

Later, the team moved to a new home stadium in Anaheim and kept the Angels name.

Chicago White Sox

Chicago White Sox
Dan Ryan at 35th Street
Chicago, IL 60616

Team Colors: Red, White, and Navy Blue
Year Founded: 1900—Chicago White Stockings
Arena: Comiskey Park
Seating Capacity: 44,432

ALTHOUGH THERE'S A simple explanation as to why the Chicago baseball club changed their team name, the White Sox organization has their own theory—a different one.

Chicago White Sox officials say the club was founded in 1900 under the name of Chicago White Stockings. But two years later, in 1902, local sports writers Sy Sanborn and Earl Green shortened the team name to "White Sox" while covering the team's away games. They came up with the nickname because the formal name was too awkward and lengthy for fitting headlines.

However, another explanation is given in a recent American League Baseball program. It states, "The team was first called the White Stockings, but the National League objected because their team in the Windy City had once used that nickname earlier; so owner Charles Comiskey shortened the name to Chicago White Sox and thumbed his nose at the rival league."

For a short period of time in the early 1920's, the team was unofficially known as the Black Sox. The name was given to the team after eight members of the 1919 White Sox were accused of conspiring to fix the World Series. After the Reds defeated the Sox in five out of eight games, a grand jury investigation indicted the players involved. Before they were brought to trial, they were banned for life from Major League Baseball. *(The Chicago White Sox are planning a new 45,000 seat stadium.)*

Cleveland Indians

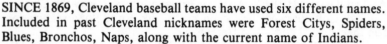

Cleveland Indians
The Stadium
Boudreau Boulevard
Cleveland, OH 44114

Team Colors: Blue and Red
Year Founded: 1869—Cleveland Forest Citys
Stadium: Cleveland Stadium
Seating Capacity: 74,208

SINCE 1869, Cleveland baseball teams have used six different names. Included in past Cleveland nicknames were Forest Citys, Spiders, Blues, Bronchos, Naps, along with the current name of Indians.

In 1869, the team was named "Forest Citys" since Cleveland was recognized as the forest city because of its thousands of beautiful trees.

Just 20 years later, 1889, the Cleveland club was comprised of many tall and skinny baseball players. So management decided to accent their wiry characteristics and renamed the team the Spiders.

In 1900, the team once again received a new name—this time the Blues, which symbolized the team's bright blue uniforms.

The team was renamed only two years later as the players disliked the effeminate name of Bluebirds and voted for a more aggressive name. Bronchos was declared the new name.

In 1903, the club was given still another nickname. The team discarded the bright blue uniforms and a local newspaper sponsored a contest to choose a new name for the team. "Naps" was the winning entry chosen in honor of baseball great Napoleon Lajoie.

In 1913, another name was chosen by team officials. The new name of Indians was announced. The name was selected to honor former Cleveland player Luis Francis Sockalexis, who was the first American Indian to play in the Major Leagues. The "Chief," as he was known during his three years with the team, had passed away in 1913.

The Indians finally came up with a name they liked and the team name has not been changed since.

Detroit Tigers

Detroit Tigers
Tiger Stadium
Detroit, MI 48216

Team Colors: Navy Blue and Orange
Year Founded: 1895
Stadium: Tiger Stadium
Seating Capacity: 52,687

Although credit for the name Tigers was originally given to George Stallings, manager for the Detroit baseball team of the Western League in 1896, later evidence shows an unidentified writer with the Detroit Free Press first used the name in 1895.

Stallings apparently took credit for the name when he dressed his players in black-and-brown stockings, which reminded him of "tiger stripes."

The Free Press, on the other hand, had called them Tigers before Stallings was manager and before the players were dressed in striped stockings.

The Detroit baseball team had earlier been called the Detroits, the Wolverines (a name associated today with the University of Michigan), and at times the Creams in years prior to 1895.

The Creams nickname broke into print in 1894, the year Detroit entered the Western Baseball League. This nickname was coined by G. A. Van Derbeck, a sportswriter from Los Angeles, who referred to the group of Detroit players as "what is purported to be the cream of California baseball players" which may have accounted for the name.

Kansas City Royals

Kansas City Royals
P. O. Box 1969
Kansas City, MO 64141

Team Colors: Royal Blue and White
Year Founded: 1969
Stadium: Royals Stadium
Seating Capacity: 40,635

IN 1968, the newly-formed Kansas City baseball club asked the public to submit a name for its new American League franchise.

Out of 17,000 suggestions, club officers chose Royals, which was selected on the basis of originality and logic.

The winner: Sanford Porte, of Overland Park, Kansas submitted: "Kansas City's new baseball team should be called the Royals because of Missouri's billion dollar livestock income, Kansas City's position as the nation's leading stocker and feeder market and the nationally known American Royal parade and pageant.

"The team colors of royal blue and white would be in harmony with the state bird, the bluebird, the state flag, the old Kansas City Blues baseball team, and our current hockey team."

Other suggested nicknames included: Mules, Steers, Bluebirds, Cowpokes, Studs, and Blues.

What did Porte get for his winning Royals suggestion?

An all-expense paid trip for two to the Major League All-Star game the following July at the Houston Astrodome.

Animal nicknames are big. These include Bruins, Rams, Broncos, Colts, Bengals, Tigers, Lions, Cubs, Bears, Bucks, and Bulls.

Milwaukee Brewers

Milwaukee Brewers
Milwaukee County Stadium
Milwaukee, WI 53214

Team Colors: Blue and Yellow
Year Founded: 1969—Seattle Pilots
Stadium: Milwaukee County Stadium
Seating Capacity: 53,192

WHEN THE BANKRUPT SEATTLE PILOTS came to Milwaukee on April 1, 1970, just a few days before a new professional baseball season got underway, the Milwaukee Baseball Club chose the name Brewers. The name was selected to represent Milwaukee, the "Beer Capitol of the World."

The name Brewers had been used earlier for a Milwaukee minor league baseball team in the early part of the century. It had been selected as a tribute to the city's long association with the brewing industry.

In 1970, the new team's logo featured "Bernie Brewer," a beer barreled figure featuring a barrel for a body, and a beer spigot for a nose. "Bernie" was dressed in a Milwaukee Brewer uniform and was posed in the official logo swinging a bat, which represented the team's strong offensive ability.

In 1978, the Brewers started a new era by hiring Vice President/General Manager Harry Dalton and Field Manager George Bamberger. This new period also brought new uniforms and a new logo.

Brewers fans became involved in a month-long contest to design a new team logo. Out of 2,000 entries, Tom Meindel of Eau Claire, Wisconsin, won the grand prize of $2,000 with his winning entry.

The Brewer logo combines the lower case "m" and "b," which represent the team initials together to form a baseball mitt and ball.

A nickname growth area seems to be the military, industry and space complex. Such names are Jets, Bullets, Supersonics, Astros, and Rockets.

Minnesota Twins

Minnesota Twins
501 Chicago Avenue
Minneapolis, MN 55415

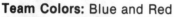

Team Colors: Blue and Red
Year Founded: 1901—Washington Senators
Stadium: Hubert H. Humphrey Metrodome
Seating Capacity: 54,711

WHEN THE WASHINGTON SENATORS moved to Minnesota in the fall of 1960, team officials chose the team name of Twin Cities Twins. This name was selected to honor the twin cities of Minneapolis and St. Paul, which are divided by the Mississippi River.

The team prepared for the 1961 season by ordering brand new uniforms for the club. The uniform included Twins in script type across the chest and a superimposed TC on the cap which represented "Twin Cities."

But before the season began, team president Calvin Griffith got a new idea. As long as the team was straying away from the standard of naming the club after one city, then why not name the team after the whole state of Minnesota?

After celebrating their 25th year in Minneapolis, club officials designed a new logo to symbolize a new era and to overcome the confusion caused by use of three previous team logos.

New York Yankees

New York Yankees
Yankee Stadium
Bronx, NY 10451

Team Colors: Navy Blue and White
Year Founded: 1903—New York Highlanders
Stadium: Yankee Stadium
Seating Capacity: 57,545

THE NEW YORK YANKEES, one of the most consistently winning baseball teams in the Major Leagues, joined the American League in 1903. This was two years after the league began.

When the franchise was formed in 1903, Joseph Gordon was named team president. The new team's new ball park was to be built on top of Washington Heights, which was the highest elevated point in Manhattan.

Someone noted that one of the most famous regiments in the British Army was known as Gordon's Highlanders. This was thought to be a fitting name since it coincided with both the playing field and the name of the team president.

The name was never popular with the fans or the layout editors of local newspapers, as it was nearly impossible in those days to squeeze an 11-letter nickname into a one-column headline.

Although both Highlanders and Hilltoppers were often used, a newspaper headline writer first used New York Yankees in 1909. The Yankee name originated in this era of nationalism when the term was often used to refer to Americans.

All three names were used until after World War I, when Yankees became the official name of the New York club.

Nicknames attuned to history include the Yankees, Phillies, Knickerbockers, 76ers, Nuggets, Trail Blazers, 49ers, Islanders, Kings, and Royals.

Oakland A's

Oakland A's
Oakland-Almeda County Stadium
Oakland, CA 94621

Team Colors: Green and Gold
Year Founded: 1900—Philadelphia Athletics
Arena: Oakland Coliseum
Seating Capacity: 57,545

PROFESSIONAL BASEBALL originated in Philadelphia in 1900, when Connie Mack fielded a team in the new American League. The appropriate name of Philadelphia Athletics was given to the club. However, it was used not as a nickname, but as the official team name since "Philadelphia" was the name of the already established National League team.

Though the name had been used by other teams in the past, it is believed it had been adopted because it was a sporty-sounding name no one else was using locally.

After 55 seasons and nine American League pennants, the team moved to Kansas City in 1955. However, the move to the midwest did not affect the name and the team was known as the Kansas City Athletics.

Yet again the team did not feel at home. The Athletics moved to Oakland in 1968. Although the team still goes by the official name of Oakland Athletics, it prefers the shortened version of Oakland A's since their shift to the west coast.

Seattle Mariners

Seattle Mariners
P. O. Box 4100
Seattle, WA 98104

Team Colors: Blue and Gold
Year Founded: 1976
Stadium: Seattle Kingdome
Seating Capacity: 59,438

AFTER THE SEATTLE PILOTS moved to Milwaukee to form the Brewers at the start of the 1970 season, the city was without representation in Major League Baseball for six years. In 1976, Seattle was granted an American League franchise for the following season.

Club officials held a contest to name their new baseball team. Over 15,000 entries were submitted which included some 600 different names.

On August 24, 1976, the new team name of Seattle Mariners was declared the winner by the team owners. The essay written by winner Roger Szmodis read, ''I've selected Mariners because of the natural associaton between the sea and Seattle and her people, who have been challenged and rewarded by it.''

Texas Rangers

Texas Rangers
P. O. Box 1111
Arlington, TX 76010

Team Colors: Red, White, and Blue
Year Founded: 1961—2nd Washington Senators
Stadium: Arlington Stadium
Seating Capacity: 41,284

AFTER THE WASHINGTON SENATORS moved to Minnesota in 1960, residents of the nation's capitol, feeling a need for a Major League franchise, were granted an American League club the following year. The team was again named Washington Senators after the United States Congress which meets in Washington, D. C.

The second version of baseball's Senators did not last as long as the original team. The team was moved to Dallas-Fort Worth, Texas, in 1971 and would play in Arlington, located between the two cities.

A public contest was held to name the new American League club. The name Texas Rangers was selected as the winner after the famed long-standing law enforcement agency whose men roamed Texas in the 1800s.

The name Rangers was previously used by a minor league baseball team located in Texas.

Toronto Blue Jays

Toronto Blue Jays
Box 7777, Adelaide St. Post Office
Toronto, Ontario M5C 2K7

Team Colors: Red, White, and Light Blue
Year Founded: 1976
Stadium: Exhibition Stadium
Seating Capacity: 43,737

LIKE MANY other professional sports franchises, the Toronto Blue Jays of the American League also received their nickname via a contest among fans.

After being accepted to Major League Baseball on March 12, 1976, the club organized a "Name the Team" contest in which the fans would suggest team names. On August 12, the team's board of directors chose Toronto Blue Jays as the name of the new American League expansion team. The name was chosen because of the great number of these birds in the provincial area surrounding the city of Toronto.

Because 154 people submitted the Blue Jays name, a drawing was held to determine the official winner. For his winning entry, Dr. William Mills of Etobicoke, Ontario, won a pair of season tickets for the 1977 season along with an all-expense paid trip for him and his family to the Blue Jays' spring training camp in Dunedin, Florida.

The Blue Jays logo—one of the most unique in professional baseball—was created by Savage Sloan, Ltd. The logo depicts a stylized Blue Jay on a red baseball outline with an imposing red maple leaf. It features two shades of blue and red.

It was selected to represent three points of the club's identity: "the team name, baseball, and the fact that the team is Canadian."

Bird nicknames include Falcons, Seahawks, Orioles, Cardinals, Hawks, Blue Jays, Eagles, and Falcons.

MAJOR LEAGUE BASEBALL®

National League
Major League Baseball

Atlanta Braves

Atlanta Braves
P. O. Box 4064
Atlanta, GA 30302

Team Colors: Red, White, and Blue
Year Founded: 1876—Boston Red Stockings
Stadium: Atlanta-Fulton County Stadium
Seating Capacity: 52,785

SINCE THE NATIONAL LEAGUE was founded in 1876, the Braves franchise has been a solid member of the league. But over the last 100-plus years, there have been 11 different names for this charter team of National League baseball.

During the team's first 35 years of existence, the official team name was changed on the average every four years.

When the club was formed in 1876, the team was known as the Boston Red Stockings. During the next four years, the team would also be called Reds, Red Caps, and Nationals.

In 1891, the name was again changed to Boston Beaneaters, named after Boston's nickname of "Beantown," and stayed that way until

1906. For the 1907 season, the name was changed once again to Boston Doves.

In 1910, the club was renamed again, this time as the Boston Rustlers.

In 1911, James E. Gaffney, a political "brave" from New York's Tammany Hall, bought the team and named it the Boston Braves. The Braves name has been with the club ever since, except for a five year stint in 1935-1940 when the team was referred to as the Boston Bees.

After a dismal 1952 season in Boston, the team was moved to Milwaukee, Wisconsin. The name remained the same as the team was known as the "Milwaukee Braves."

Prior to the 1966 season, the team moved once again—this time to Atlanta, Georgia, and the team was now known as the Atlanta Braves. The name has remained the same ever since.

Chicago Cubs

Chicago Cubs
Wrigley Field
Chicago, IL 60613

Team Colors: Red, White, and Blue
Year Founded: 1876—Chicago White Stockings
Stadium: Wrigley Field
Seating Capacity: 37,272

EVER SINCE THE CREATION of the National League in 1876, Chicago has fielded a baseball team. William A. Hulbert, the first president of the Chicago club, was credited for organizing the National League.

He drafted a league constitution and by-laws in 1875. To this day, almost all of the rules drawn by Hulbert are still in use.

Although nicknames were not official in the early years of the league, the Chicago team was first called the White Stockings. After 1890, the most popular names for the club were Colts and Orphans.

Yet on March 27, 1902, a newspaper writer used the name Chicago Cubs while searching for a short name to fit a headline. In 1907, Chicago Cubs was announced as the official team name and it has remained the same ever since.

Cincinnati Reds

Cincinnati Reds
100 Riverfront Stadium
Cincinnati, OH 45202

Team Colors: Red and White
Year Founded: 1869—Red Stockings
Stadium: Riverfront Stadium
Seating Capacity: 52,392

THE CINCINNATI REDS, originally known as the Cincinnati Red Stockings and named after their colorful uniform stockings, first began professional play in 1869. The team won 130 consecutive baseball games in their first two seasons before losing to the Brooklyn Atlantics in 1870.

When the National League was founded in 1876, the Red Stockings became a charter member. However, they dropped out in 1881 when the league banned sale of beer from the park. The club became a member of the American Association and later joined the Union Association. But in 1890, they rejoined the National League.

The name of the club was later shortened just to Reds. Yet in the 1950s along with Joe McCarthy's Communist scare, the name was thought by some to be synonymous with the Communists, and the club officially changed the team name to the Redlegs. However, the team name was later changed back to Reds.

Houston Astros

Houston Astros
P. O. Box 288
Houston, TX 77001-0288

Team Colors: Navy Blue, Red, Orange, Yellow, and White
Year Founded: 1960—Houston Colt .45s
Stadium: Houston Astrodome
Seating Capacity: 45,000

ON OCTOBER 17, 1960, Judge Roy Hofheinz was awarded a National League baseball franchise. The new club, which took the field for the first time in 1962, was named in January of 1961 during an announcement at the site of the new multi-sports playing facility.

On the site of Hofheinz's "Astrodomain"—as it was called—Judge Hofheinz celebrated at the groundbreaking ceremony by firing a Colt .45 pistol into the ground. The new team was named after the powerful weapon and the club was named the Houston Colt .45s. The reasoning behind the name was that the pistol that had won the West was a fitting name for Texas' first major league baseball team.

In April of 1965, the Astrodome was finished and the Colt .45s became the Houston Astros as the first indoor baseball games were played in professional baseball.

Yet having an indoor playing field wasn't what Hofheinz and the Astros expected. In an exhibition game with the Baltimore Orioles, worried Astros manager Lum Harris commented, "You just can't follow the ball. We may be here all day tomorrow trying to get this game finished."

The day was definitely an unforgettable one for the players. "I'm not going back into the outfield without a batting helmet!", shouted Baltimore's Boog Powell after misjudging a pop fly in the third inning.

Houston officials did not really take the problem seriously until Paul Blair of Baltimore hit a routine fly ball to the outfield and ran around each of the bases before the Astro outfielders found the ball. "We definitely have a problem," stated Hofheinz. With no other possible solution, a coat of paint was applied to the roof of the dome.

That was not the end of the Astro's problems, however. Hofheinz had earlier financed a study at Texas A&M University to determine if the dome could have a natural grass playing field. After studies showed it would be possible, grass was brought in and laid down.

However, when the roof was painted, the grass began to wither and die. Therefore, Hofheinz had a synthetic "grass" made of nylon called Astroturf laid on the field. Soon afterward, many other professional sports organizations learned from this experience that artifical turf was more economical and durable than natural grass.

Los Angeles Dodgers

Los Angeles Dodgers
1000 Elysian Park Avenue
Los Angeles, CA 90012-1199

Team Colors: Blue and White
Year Founded: 1890—Brooklyn Dodgers
Stadium: Dodger Stadium
Seating Capacity: 56,000

BROOKLYN, NEW YORK, had long been noted for its high interest in baseball even in the pre-Civil War era. While the city had strong baseball clubs such as the Atlantics, Eckfords, and Excelsiors, they did not actually have professional baseball until 1884 when a local team joined the American Association.

In 1890, Brooklyn organized a club in the National League which became known as the "Brooklyn Trolley Dodgers" because of the great maze of streetcars in the borough of Brooklyn.

The "Trolley Dodgers" name, shortened to Dodgers, remained permanent. From 1899-1905, the team name was changed to "Superbas" and from 1914-1931 the team was often referred to as the "Robins."

Although the team was moved to Los Angeles in 1958, the Dodger name has remained the same ever since.

Montreal Expos

Montreal Expos
P.O. Box 500
Station "M"
Montreal, Quebec H1V 3P2

Team Colors: Red, White, and Blue
Year Founded: 1968
Stadium: Olympic Stadium
Seating Capacity: 58,838

FOLLOWING THE GREAT SUCCESS of the 1967 World's Fair held in Montreal, Canada, the city was awarded a baseball team in the National League.

The Montreal World's Fair, often referred to as Expo '67, was so popular among the people of Montreal that the baseball team was named after it. The team was named Montreal Expos in honor of the world-reknowned Fair that brought international attention to Montreal.

The Expo team logo is made up of three distinct letters which can often be overlooked. Looking at the complete logo, the largest letter is the stylized "M" standing for Montreal. On the lower left side of the emblem is a red lower case "e" for Expos and on the righthand side is a blue lower case "b" for baseball, which together form the "M."

The Expos were the first team in major league baseball to be formed outside the United States—in an area of eastern Canada where the official language is French and not English.

New York Mets

New York Mets
Shea Stadium
Flushing, NY 11368

Team Colors: Blue, Orange, and White
Year Founded: 1961
Stadium: Shea Stadium
Seating Capacity: 55,300

"THE NAME IS METS...just plain Mets," the press release stated announcing the Big Apple's new National League expansion team on May 8, 1961.

The name Mets was chosen by club owner Mrs. Joan Payson based on five specific points. Payson stated that it met public and press acceptance, it was closely related to the team's corporate name (Metropolitan Baseball Club, Inc.), it was descriptive of the New York metropolitan area, it had a brevity that delighted copywriters everywhere, and the name had historical background—dating back to the 19th century New York Metropolitans of the American Association.

Other team names considered by Payson were Avengers, Continentals, Rebels, Skyliners, NYBs, and Burros—for New York's five borroughs. Jets and Islanders were also in the running, names which later were used by professional New York football and hockey teams, respectively.

Philadelphia Phillies

Philadelphia Phillies
P. O. Box 7575
Philadelphia, PA 19101

Team Colors: Crimson and White
Year Founded: 1883
Stadium: Veterans Stadium
Seating Capacity: 65,454

PHILADELPHIA PHILLIES have the oldest team name in the National League part of Major League baseball.

The first game played in the National League's history was played on April 22, 1876, in Philadelphia, Pennsylvania, as the Philadelphia Athletics were playing Boston. However, the Athletics folded before the end of the first season so the "baseball-crazed" Quaker City was without representation in professional baseball.

Deciding the city needed a National League franchise, Alfred J. Reach purchased the Worchester Brown Stockings of Massachusetts prior to the 1883 season. The team was renamed Philadelphia Phillies, as a takeoff on Philadelphia or Philly, as the city was often referred to in those days.

With only limited seating capacity at the Phillies home field, Recreation Park, more seats were needed if the team was to survive.

The Phillies moved into a new ball park in 1887, Baker Bowl, which could seat over 15,000.

One of baseball's biggest disasters hit Baker Bowl in 1903. After a spectator saw a nearby fire from his seat in the top row of the bleachers, fans rushed to the top row to get a better view of the flames. As the left field bleachers collapsed, 12 people were killed in the fall and 232 were seriously injured.

In 1910, team owner Horace Fogel began a campaign to rename the club. Fogel stated, "The name Phillies is too trite and Quakers (as the team was often referred to) stands for peaceful people who will dodge a fight.

"We're going to fight. Why don't you fellas call the club the 'Live Wires'?"

Fogel's efforts were not to become reality as the press never printed the suggested name in the papers.

In 1943, the team was sold to R.R.M. Carpenter, Jr. To stimulate interest, a contest was held to find a new nickname for the team. During the 1944 and 1945 seasons, the team was known as the Blue Jays, although Phillies was still declared the official team name.

Interest in the nickname contest died out and the Phillies were to continue as Philadelphia's entry in the National League—a tradition that goes all the way back to 1883.

Pittsburgh Pirates

Pittsburgh Pirates
600 Stadium Circle
Pittsburgh, PA 15212

Team Colors: Gold and Black
Year Founded: 1876—Pittsburgh Alleghenies
Stadium: Three Rivers Stadium
Seating Capacity: 54,499

PROFESSIONAL BASEBALL was brought to Pittsburgh in 1876 as the Pittsburgh Alleghenies played their first season. The team name, Alleghenies, was named after the Allegheny River that runs through Pittsburgh.

In 1882, the club joined the American Association, the rival of the National League. After five years of success, the team was accepted by the National League and played their first NL season in 1887.

Because the franchise could not pay very high salaries to its players, many of the team stars transferred to the Players (Brotherhood) League in 1890. The League folded shortly afterward and players were ordered to return to their original teams.

After the players returned to the National League, the Pittsburgh club was accused of illegally "pirating" a player from the Philadelphia team and received the nickname of Pittsburgh Pirates. The name has remained the same ever since.

On June 30, 1909, the Pirates began playing at Forbes Field, the first steel-structured stadium in Major League history.

St. Louis Cardinals

St. Louis Cardinals
250 Stadium Plaza
St. Louis, MO 63102-1722

Team Colors: Red and White
Year Founded: 1899
Stadium: Busch Memorial Stadium
Seating Capacity: 51,392

AROUND THE turn of the century, the St. Louis baseball club owner decided to throw away the team's drab brown uniforms and outfit his players in new uniforms which featured bright red trim.

A woman saw the new baseball uniforms and commented, "what a lovely shade of Cardinal."

Willie McHale, a sportswriter for the St. Louis Republic newspaper, overheard the lady's comment and started referring to the team as the St. Louis Cardinals. From that time on, the baseball club used the name officially.

In the early 1920s, an Illinois woman sent general manager Branch Rickey a drawing of the Cardinal perched on a bat, which was adopted as the team's logo and eventually used on the team uniforms.

Many of the more aggressive nicknames are found with older franchises, such as Pirates and Tigers. However, more modern-day aggressive nicknames include Flames, Sabres, Mavericks, and Bullets.

San Diego Padres

San Diego Padres
9449 Friars Road
P. O. Box 2000
San Diego, CA 92108-1771

Team Colors: Brown and Yellow
Year Founded: 1969
Stadium: Jack Murphy Stadium
Seating Capacity: 58,000

THE SAN DIEGO PADRES nickname originated from a triple A farm club and was later adopted by the new National League franchise upon entering the league in 1969.

When the minor league Padres first began in San Diego in 1935, a newspaper contest was held to select a name for the new baseball club. Padres was selected as the winner in honor of the Spanish padres (priests) who built a chain of missions throughout California during the early 1800s.

When San Diego was awarded a Major League franchise in 1969, the name Padres was taken as the official team name of the club.

San Francisco Giants

San Francisco Giants
Candlestick Park
San Francisco, CA 94124

Team Colors: Black, Orange, and White
Year Founded: 1883—New York Gothams
Stadium: Candlestick Park
Seating Capacity: 58,000

DURING THE 1880s, baseball became very popular in the New York City area. The "Gothams" were brought to New York in time for the 1883 National League season by factory owner John B. Day and local sports figure Jim Mutrie, who also organized the New York Metropolitans of the American Association.

The Giants name was adopted after a quote by team manager Jim Mutrie in 1886. During mid-season, after a great victory that moved the Gothams into second place behind Cap Anson's immortal Chicago White Stockings, Mutrie proclaimed to his team, "My big fellows! My Giants! We are the People!"

Based on the manager's quote, from that point on the club was officially named Giants.

Although the Giants moved to San Francisco in July of 1957, the team name remained the same due to the great popularity and success which the baseball team had enjoyed in New York.

American Football Conference
National Football League

Buffalo Bills

Buffalo Bills
One Bills Drive
Orchard Park, NY 14127

Team Colors: Blue and Red
Year Founded: 1946—All American Football Conference
Stadium: Rich Stadium
Seating Capacity: 80,020

THE BUFFALO BILLS name was created in a contest to pick a nickname for the new football club that would begin its first season in the All-American Football Conference in 1946.

The winner was Jimmy Dyson, who won a silver tea set for submitting the Bills nickname. The essay that Dyson submitted for his entry mentioned Buffalo Bill, the famous hero of the West, who was part of the American Frontier. He also stated that the new team sponsored by Frontier Oil (which was owner Jim Breuil's company) was opening a new frontier in sports in Western New York. Hence the name, the Buffalo Bills.

The Bills kept the name upon entering the American Football League in 1959 and have used the name ever since.

Cincinnati Bengals

Cincinnati Bengals
200 Riverfront Stadium
Cincinnati, OH 45202

Team Colors: Orange, Black, and White
Year Founded: 1967—American Football League
Stadium: Riverfront Stadium
Seating Capacity: 59,754

THE CINCINNATI BENGALS of the National Football League were named after a former pro football team by the same name that played from 1937-1941.

Cincinnati had also once had an NFL team in 1933 called the Cincinnati Reds, but the team folded after seven straight Sundays of rain.

Coach and general manager Paul Brown stated, "If we can pick up a thread of tradition, we think it's good. We feel at home with the name Bengals. And in naming them Bengals, we mean the tigers, not the lancers."

Many possible team names were suggested to the Post and Times-Star. The most popular name submitted was Buckeyes, which was not the favorite among team officials. "That name is already used by Ohio State," commented Brown. "Also, I feel we are part of a four-state area, not just one state."

Other names suggested were Krauts, Celts, and Romans.

Cleveland Browns

Cleveland Browns
Cleveland Stadium
Cleveland, OH 44114

Team Colors: Seal Brown, Burnt Orange, and White
Year Founded: 1946—All American Football Conference
Stadium: Cleveland Municipal Stadium
Seating Capacity: 80,322

TO FIND a name for the Cleveland football club, team officials decided to run a contest to name the team in May, 1945, with a $1,000 war bond going to the winner.

Navy sailor John J. Harnett was declared the winner with his entry of the Cleveland Panthers. This name was chosen because it could be easily animated for promotional use and was a name around which a symbol could easily be created. Yet shortly afterward, the club became aware that a semi-pro football team near Cleveland was already using the Panther name. Coach Paul Brown looked into the operation of the semi-pro team and not only found out such a team existed, but that it was a chronic loser.

"Forget the name," Brown said. "I won't have my team associated with a loser, not in any sense of the word." So, the club ran another contest for suggesting a team name.

"Joe Louis was the best known champion at that time, and we received a lot of entries suggesting we name the team the Brown Bombers. So we decided to shorten the name and call the team the Browns," stated Brown. Or was it just a coincidence that the name was the same as the team's coach and general manager?

The team received double the amount of publicity and awarded another war bond to William E. Thompson who was declared winner of the second contest.

The team played four years in the All-American Football Conference and then joined the National Football League in 1950. (You'll note that the Browns are the only remaining National Football League team to go with the old-fashioned helmets which feature no team logo).

Colorful nicknames include Red Sox, Blues, Browns, Reds, and White Sox.

Denver Broncos

Denver Broncos
5700 Logan Street
Denver, CO 80216

Team Colors: Orange, Royal Blue, and White
Year Founded: 1959—American Football League
Stadium: Mile High Stadium
Seating Capacity: 75,103

THE DENVER BRONCOS of the National Football League, began professional football as charter members of the American Football League in 1959.

A contest among the fans was held to name Denver's new AFL franchise immediately following their acceptance to the league. The name of Denver Broncos was chosen as the one that would best suit the team. The name had earlier been used by a baseball team which existed in Denver, and symbolized the toughness and determination of the west.

Bronco general manager Dean Guffring purchased the team uniforms from the defunct Copper Bowl. The colors were light brown and "barnyard brown"—as it was called by its critics.

The uniform also included incredibly ugly, vertically striped socks—unheard of in football. The players hated the socks, refused to wear them, and most players even refused to try them on. However, when Jack Faulkner took over as head coach in 1962, he burned the hideous socks at a public ceremony.

It looked as though the Denver team was "in danger of death" in its first season. The Broncos lost all five exhibition games and entered the season with little hope as just 2,600 season tickets were purchased.

A Denver area funeral home owner bought the first eight season tickets—maybe figuring he would get some business from a quick demise of the team.

Yet the Broncos were the first AFL team to win a game—beating the Boston Patriots 13-10 in a Friday night game in Boston—the day before the rest of the league went into action. However, it was not a successful season for the team, as they finished with a record of 4 wins, 9 losses and 1 tie.

When Denver was accepted into the NFL in 1969, they continued horsin' around under the same Bronco name.

Indianapolis Colts

Indianapolis Colts
P. O. Box 24100
7001 W. 56th Street
Indianapolis, IN 46254

Team Colors: Blue and White
Year Founded: 1946—Miami Seahawks (A.A.F.C.)
Stadium: Hoosier Dome
Seating Capacity: 60,127

THE CITY OF BALTIMORE received its first professional football team on December 28, 1946, when the bankrupt Miami Seahawks of the All-American Football Conference were purchased by a group of area citizens.

Because "Seahawks" did not fit in with Baltimore's image, a contest was held and the name Baltimore Colts was declared the winner.

In 1950, the All-American Football Conference and National Football League merged and the Colts played their first NFL season the same year. After a record of a single win and 11 losses, the team folded because of its bad financial situation.

After three full seasons without professional football, the original Dallas Texans were moved to Baltimore on January 23, 1953. The team adopted the name of Baltimore Colts that was previously used. However, the team stuck with the colors of blue and white which had been used by the Texans.

On March 29, 1984, the Baltimore Colts moved to Indianapolis, Indiana, but remained under the same name.

Houston Oilers

Houston Oilers
P.O. Box 1516
Houston, TX 77251-1516

Team Colors: Columbia Blue, Scarlet, and White
Year Founded: 1960—American Football League
Arena: Houston Astrodome
Seating Capacity: 50,496

K.S. "BUD" ADAMS, the founder of the Houston Oilers and co-founder of the American Football League along with Lamar Hunt, is recognized as a pioneer in professional football.

Adams incorporated ADA Oil Company in 1947, a forerunner of Adam Resources and Energy, Inc. With his profits from the oil business, Adams purchased a football franchise in the American Football League on August 3, 1959.

On October 31, 1959, Adams announced the team name as the Houston Oilers—"for sentimental and social reasons." Undoubtedly, Adams named his club after his business that allowed him to buy the team.

The Oilers won the first two AFL championships and lost the third to the Dallas Texans in sudden-death overtime. After these three championship games, the team started to fall apart. From 1963-1966, the team won only 17 games while being defeated in 39 contests.

The Oilers played in three different stadiums and were coached by six different men during the 1960's. They bounced between Jeppesen Field and Rice University before settling at the Astrodome.

Kansas City Chiefs

Kansas City Chiefs
One Arrowhead Drive
Kansas City, MO 64129

Team Colors: Red, Gold, and White
Year Founded: 1959—Dallas Texans (A.F.L.)
Arena: Arrowhead Stadium
Seating Capacity: 78,198

THE DALLAS TEXANS, one of the original American Football League franchises, was established by Lamar Hunt in 1959. Hunt was one of the founders and leaders of the new league.

The team was named Texans by Hunt, a hometown native of Dallas. They were very successful in the AFL, winning the league championship in 1962, yet lost fan support to the crosstown Dallas Cowboys of the National Football League. Thus, the team was moved to Kansas City, Missouri, in 1963.

The Kansas City football team held a contest for naming the team in 1963, and Chiefs was chosen by Hunt as the best suggestion.

After Kansas City defeated Minnesota in Super Bowl IV, the NFL allowed several AFL teams to merge into their league. All of the teams were divided into two distinct conferences in the NFL, the American Football Conference and the National Football Conference.

Los Angeles Raiders

Los Angeles Raiders
332 Center Street
El Segundo, CA 90245

Team Colors: Silver and Black
Year Founded: 1960—Oakland Raiders (A.F.L.)
Arena: Los Angeles Coliseum
Seating Capacity: 92,516

THE CITY OF OAKLAND received its first professional football franchise on January 30, 1960, following the withdrawal of the Minneapolis-St. Paul club from the newly born American Football League.

Soon after the team's admittance to the league, a lengthy formal name was developed for the team—The Metropolitan Oakland Area Football Club. This name was felt by team officials to be too long for public use.

The Oakland Chamber of Commerce suggested a contest be held to name the team. The winning entry was Oakland Señors. However, team officials vetoed that choice and decided to select the name themselves and announced the new Oakland Raiders team name.

The first three seasons were tough for the Raiders with a record of only 9 wins against 33 losses. From 1960 to 1966, the homeless Raiders virtually bounced between Kezar Stadium to Candlestick Park to Frank Youell Field before settling in their permanent home, the 53,000 seat Oakland-Almeda County Coliseum.

Yet the fierce Raiders would not give up their fight for victory. Toward the end of the 1960's, the team came together with an AFC championship team and three consecutive division championships which led them on their way to becoming one of professional sports' winningest teams.

In 1982, after much controversy, the Raiders moved to Los Angeles, and became known as the Los Angeles Raiders. *(The Los Angeles Raiders will soon move into a 65,000 seat stadium in Irwindale, Calif.).*

Among the villians of history, nicknames include Pirates, Buccaneers, Vikings, Raiders, Giants, Warriors, Sabres, and even the Devils.

Miami Dolphins

Miami Dolphins
4770 Biscayne Boulevard
Suite 1440
Miami, FL 33137

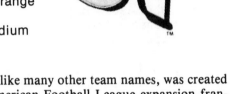

Team Colors: Blue and Orange
Year Founded: 1965
Stadium: Joe Robbie Stadium
Seating Capacity: 74,993

THE MIAMI DOLPHINS, like many other team names, was created in a public contest. The American Football League expansion franchise contest in 1965 attracted almost 20,000 names.

The bottlenosed dolphin, which is the team's mascot, is an intelligent creature with an irresistible built-in grin. As observed by Plutarch 1,900 years ago, "the dolphin is the only creature who loves man for his own sake."

"The dolphin is one of the fastest and smartest creatures of the sea," team owner Joseph Robbie commented while announcing the team name. "Dolphins can attack and kill a shark or a whale. Sailors say bad luck will come to anyone who harms one of them."

Other name suggestions included: Mariners, Marauders, Mustangs, Missiles, Moons, Sharks, and Suns. Mrs. Robert Swanson of West Miami, Florida, won two lifetime passes to Dolphin games with her winning entry of Miami Dolphins.

New England Patriots

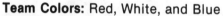

New England Patriots
Sullivan Stadium
Route One
Foxboro, MA 02035-9801

Team Colors: Red, White, and Blue
Year Founded: 1960—Boston Patriots (A.F.L.)
Stadium: Schaefer Stadium
Seating Capacity: 61,297

WILLIAM SULLIVAN, JR., had a dream. His dream was that Boston would someday have its own professional football team.

In 1959, his dream came true. Sullivan received a phone call from Lamar Hunt asking if Boston would like to field a team in the newly-born American Football League.

Immediately, Sullivan set about forming a syndicate of nine equal owners. In an effort to involve the fans, Sullivan initiated a public contest entitled "Name Your Football Franchise."

The name Boston Patriots was selected in honor of the history of the 18th Century colonists who helped declare independence from Britain. The team colors were chosen as red, white, and blue, the same as the American flag.

In 1970, the American Football League and the National League merged. After finishing with a record of 2 wins and 12 losses in 1970, the team was moved to Foxboro, Massachusetts, and Schaefer Stadium.

Since the team was no longer stationed in Boston, the name was changed to New England Patriots.

New York Jets

New York Jets
598 Madison Avenue
New York, NY 10022

Team Colors: Kelly Green and White
Year Founded: 1960—New York Titans (A.F.L.)
Arena: Shea Stadium
Seating Capacity: 60,372

THE NEW YORK JETS of the National Football League were original members of the American Football League in 1960 as the New York Titans.

The team was primarily owned by radio personality Harry Wismer. However, the franchise declared bankruptcy in 1963 and it looked like the team would fold.

Yet Sonny Werblin was destined to keep the team in New York and headed a five-man syndicate to purchase the Titans for $1 million.

Immediately after the transaction, Werblin hired Weeb Ewbank as head coach and changed the team name to New York Jets. "We need a new image," said Werblin. "So we'll begin with a successful established coach and a new name—one not so grandiose."

Werblin selected the Jets name for several reasons. The country was entering the "Jet Age" or "Space Age." Also Shea Stadium, the team's new playing field, would soon be built between New York's two principal airports—LaGuardia and Idlewild (which would later be known as John F. Kennedy International). And of course, the short name could easily be used by headline writers.

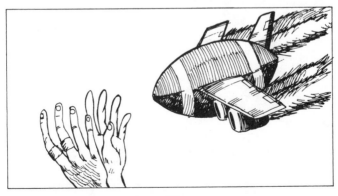

Pittsburgh Steelers

Pittsburgh Steelers
300 Stadium Circle
Pittsburgh, PA 15212

Team Colors: Black and Gold
Year Founded: 1933—Pittsburgh Pirates
Stadium: Three Rivers Stadium
Seating Capacity: 50,350

THE ORIGINAL FOOTBALL TEAM founded in 1933 by owner Art Rooney was known as the Pittsburgh Pirates, featuring the same name as the city's baseball team.

In 1940 Rooney changed the team's name to Steelers, to properly represent the city known as the "Steel Capitol of the World." The National Football League's fifth oldest team has operated under the same name ever since.

In 1963, the year the Steelers lost the National Football League title game to the New York Giants, the team adopted a new logo known as the Steelmark. This famous logo is also used by the American Iron and Steel Institute, signifying the strength and durability of both steel and the Steelers.

San Diego Chargers

San Diego Chargers
P. O. Box 20666
San Diego, CA 92120-0606

Team Colors: Royal Blue, Gold, and White
Year Founded: 1959—Los Angeles Chargers (A.F.L.)
Stadium: Jack Murphy Stadium
Seating Capacity: 52,675

BARRON HILTON, the Chargers' first owner, helped organize the American Football League in 1959. For the league's inaugural season, there were six teams: Dallas, Houston, New York, Minneapolis, Denver, and Los Angeles.

On October 27, 1959, former Notre Dame football coach and team general manager Frank Leahy announced that the new team would be called the Los Angeles Chargers. Gerald Courtney of Hollywood won an all-expense-paid trip to Mexico City and Acapulco for submitting the most appropriate team name in a contest.

During the team's first season in Los Angeles, the team finished with 10 wins and 4 losses and won the Western Division Championship with their wide-open gambling style of play. However, the presence of the L. A. Rams of the National Football League caused too much competition for the club and they moved to San Diego, California, on February 10, 1961.

Although the American Football League merged into the National Football League in 1969, the San Diego team kept the same name and logo.

Seattle Seahawks

Seattle Seahawks
5305 Lake Washington Boulevard
Kirkland, WA 98033

Team Colors: Blue, Green, and Silver
Year Founded: 1976
Stadium: Seattle Kingdome
Seating Capacity: 64,752

THE SEATTLE SEAHAWKS of the National Football League, like many other professional sports teams, obtained their nickname from their future fans.

After the NFL admitted Seattle to the League in 1974, the Seattle Professional Football club sponsored a "name the team" contest among folks in the Pacific Northwest.

Out of an amazing 20,365 suggested names, the winning entry of Seattle Seahawks was announced by team officials on June 17, 1975. In reality, the Seattle Seahawks name had been suggested by an astounding 151 fans.

"Our new name shows aggressiveness, reflects our soaring Northwest heritage, and belongs to no other major league team," commented team general manager John Thompson.

"Our name is very important to us. We wanted to do it right, and to develop a suitable name, color selection, emblem, and logo type to best represent the Northwest. Our fans have been extremely helpful, and their support is the key to the Seahawks' success."

Other names suggested by prospective name-makers were the Mariners, Skippers, Pioneers, Lumberjacks, Spacers, Sockeyes, Seagulls, and Spinnakers.

National Football Conference
National Football League

Atlanta Falcons

Atlanta Falcons
Suwanee Road at I-85
Suwanee, GA 30174

Team Colors: Red, Black, White, and Silver
Year Founded: 1965
Stadium: Atlanta-Fulton County Stadium
Seating Capacity: 60,748

AFTER GROUND was broken for the building of Atlanta-Fulton County Stadium, the city officials of Atlanta immediately began looking for a professional football team of their own.

Yet when National Football League commissioner Pete Rozelle announced there would be no further expansion of the NFL until 1967, the younger league moved in. The newly-formed American Football League quickly awarded Atlanta a franchise.

However, Rozelle then took a poll of Atlanta citizens and learned they overwhelmingly preferred an NFL club to an AFL club.

So, the Falcons were born. Rankin M. Smith, a 41-year old insurance executive was awarded an NFL franchise on June 30, 1965, for approximately $8.5 million.

The next step, however, was developing a team name. After a contest sponsored by team officials and WSB radio, Smith announced the name Atlanta Falcons at the Pittsburgh-Baltimore exhibition game on August 29.

Although the Falcons name was submitted by more than 40 contestants, Miss Julia Elliot—a high school teacher from Griffin, Georgia—was named the winner because of her essay.

Elliot's essay read, "The Falcon is proud and dignified, with great courage and fight. It never drops its prey. It's deadly and has a great sporting tradition."

Other team names submitted were: Knights, Bombers, Rebels, Crackers, Thrashers, Lancers, Firebirds, Fireballs, Thunderbirds, as well as hundreds of other suggestions.

"I hope everyone will be pleased with the judges' selection," said Smith. "I think the Atlanta Falcons is a good name and we'll do our best to make it a famous one."

Chicago Bears

Chicago Bears
P. O. Box 204
250 North Washington Road
Lake Forest, IL 60045

Team Colors: Burnt Orange, Navy, and White
Year Founded: 1920 Decatur Staleys (A.P.F.A.)
Stadium: Soldier Field
Seating Capacity: 64,124

THE CHICAGO BEARS, founded by the great George Halas in 1920, were originally the Decatur Staleys of the American Professional Football Association.

On August 17, 1920, Halas of the Staleys along with 12 other representatives met in Canton, Ohio. The meeting was held to discuss plans for organizing the American Professional Football Association which later became the National Football League.

In 1921, the Staleys moved to Chicago and became the Chicago Staleys. After Chicago won the APFA title game, A.E. Staley gave Halas $5,000 to keep the Staley team name for the following season.

Immediately following the 1921 football season, the name was changed to Chicago Bears by Halas on January 28, 1928, and the name has remained the same ever since.

The Bears nickname fit the team well. They became the "Monsters of the Midway" and were known as fierce players who played with rambunctiousness and tenacity. *(Plans are being drawn up for a new Chicago Bears stadium.)*

Dallas Cowboys

Dallas Cowboys
Cowboys Center
One Cowboys Parkway
Irving, TX 75063-4727

Team Colors: Royal Blue, Metallic Silver, and White
Year Founded: 1960
Stadium: Texas Stadium
Seating Capacity: 65,101

IN 1960 DALLAS, TEXAS, received a National Football League franchise. Team officials decided to name the new team the Dallas Rangers after the legendary Texas police force that once roamed the Lone Star state.

Shortly afterward, team general manager Tex Schramm became aware that a local minor league baseball team also went by the Rangers name.

Schramm, who did not want to interfere or cause any confusion between the two clubs, decided to call a meeting with the team's owners to rename the football team.

The meeting ended with Dallas Cowboys as the new name of the team.

A look at today's Dallas team helmets shows their logo features a star—a throwback to both the Lone Star State and also to the Texas Rangers police force.

The Dallas Cowboys were the first NFL expansion team to win a Super Bowl Championship—doing so during their eleventh season.

Detroit Lions

Detroit Lions
1200 Featherstone
P. O. Box 4200
Pontiac, MI 48057

Team Colors: Blue and Silver
Year Founded: 1930—Portsmouth Spartans
Stadium: Pontiac Silverdome
Seating Capacity: 80,638

FOR A $50 BILL, Jimmy Conzelman purchased franchise rights for a Detroit team in the National Football League in 1925. While Conzelman was the first entrepreneur of professional football in the Motor City, his success was not to last.

The team folded in 1926, then made a brief comeback in 1928 and finally died an unceremonious death in 1930.

Four years later, a successful radio station owner named George Richards decided Detroit needed a professional football team. Richards went shopping for a new football team and bought the Portsmouth Spartans of Ohio.

Upon the arrival of the Spartans in 1934, the team name was changed to the Detroit Lions.

The new name was based on the success the Detroit Tigers baseball team was having that year in their spirited fight for the American League baseball championship—which they later won, although losing to St. Louis in the World Series. As everyone knows, the Detroit baseball club's nickname is based on another jungle feline.

Team officials had wanted to call the football team the Tigers, but this might have created confusion among Motor City sports fans.

"The Lion is monarch of the jungle," stated Cy Houston, vice president and general manager of the team, "and we hope to be monarch of the league. It is our ambition to make the Lion as famous as the Detroit ball club has made the Tiger."

Copycat names include the New York Jets who came after the Mets, the Detroit Lions who came after the Tigers, and the Chicago Bears who were named after the windy city's Cubs.

Green Bay Packers

Green Bay Packers
P. O. Box 10628
Green Bay, WI 54307

Team Colors: Dark Green, Gold and White
Year Founded: 1919
Stadium: Lambeau Field, Milwaukee County Stadium
Seating Capacity: 56,267, 55,958

THE PACKERS, the National Football League team from Green Bay, Wisconsin, took on their name because of the corporation that originally paid for their equipment.

During the summer of 1919, Curly Lambeau and George Calhoun came up with the idea to start a football team in Green Bay.

Lambeau, who worked at the Indian Packing Company in Green Bay, asked the firm to provide funds for equipment. Because the uniforms and practice field were provided by the packing company, the team was named the Packers. The club has kept that name ever since, even though the corporation faded out before the first season was over.

In the team's early years, games were played in an open field with no fences or bleachers. A hat was passed among spectators at the game and the money was divided up among players after the game. Still, this was the only income the players received during the first few years.

The team was so successful the first season that two officers of the packing plant backed Lambeau in obtaining a franchise for Green Bay in the new National Football League. The Green Bay Packers became a member of the NFL in 1921, a year after the league was formed.

Green Bay is the only major professional sports team to have two home fields. Besides using Lambeau Field in Green Bay, the team also plays several home games a year 125 miles south in Milwaukee's County Stadium.

Some nicknames promote special causes. These include Packers, Steelers, Oilers, Brewers, Capitals, Nordiques, Twins, North Stars, Canadains, Canucks, Blues and Maple Leafs.

Los Angeles Rams

Los Angeles Rams
2327 West Lincoln Ave.
Anaheim, CA 92801

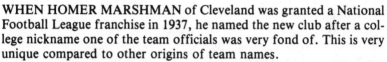

Team Colors: Royal Blue, Gold, and White
Year Founded: 1937—Cleveland Rams
Stadium: Anaheim Stadium
Seating Capacity: 69,007

WHEN HOMER MARSHMAN of Cleveland was granted a National Football League franchise in 1937, he named the new club after a college nickname one of the team officials was very fond of. This is very unique compared to other origins of team names.

There had previously been a professional football team in Cleveland in the American Football Association in 1921. The team, known as the Cleveland Indians, had folded. It was expected that Marshman would name his new club after the old team.

However, when Marshman was awarded the NFL club, he and his general manager, Buzz Wetzel, set out to find a new name.

"If there is one college team that has a name I really like, it's the Fordham Rams," commented Wetzel. After hearing this suggestion, Marshman agreed immediately, stating, "That's wonderful. That's what we'll call them. The Cleveland Rams."

In 1941, the Rams changed ownership after a poor season of 4 wins, 6 losses, and 1 tie. The team was bought by Daniel F. Reeves and Fred Levy who started their rebuilding program for the 1942 season.

After winning the NFL championship in 1945, Reeves moved the team out of the Midwest to the modern, vibrant metropolis city of Los Angeles. Although there was much controversy with the league and other team owners concerning the move west, the Rams were eventually permitted to do so; thus becoming the first professional football franchise on the west coast.

The Los Angeles Rams also started a precedent in 1948. Fred Gehrke, Ram halfback and artist, took the team's helmets home and painted the famous ram horns that would eventually become the team trademark.

During the next few seasons, Gehrke would hand paint each and every helmet with the Ram symbol, as modern printing techniques were not yet efficient.

Minnesota Vikings

Minnesota Vikings
9520 Viking Place
Eden Prairie, MN 55344

Team Colors: Purple, Gold, and White
Year Founded: 1960
Stadium: Hubert H. Humphrey Metrodome
Seating Capacity: 62,212

IN 1960, THE MINNESOTA VIKINGS became the 14th franchise in the National Football League.

When Bert Rose was hired as General Manager of the new Minnesota team in 1961, he was given the challenge to find a nickname that would well suit the new team.

"A nickname should serve a dual purpose," stated Rose on developing the team name. "It should represent an aggressive person or animal imbued with the will to win. Secondly, if possible, it is desirable to have it connote the region that the team respresents."

The team name Vikings was selected by Rose on the basis of the two points listed above. The Nordic Vikings were definitely a fearless race with their many years of victories in the British Isles and France.

Under the leadership of Erik the Red, they sailed in open boats across the Atlantic to find new lands to conquer. The Nordic people were always noted for their aggressiveness and desire to win.

Minnesota is an area rich with Nordic background, so the Vikings illustrate a name that many people of Minnesota call their home.

The original Viking team logo was drawn by Los Angeles Times sports cartoonist Karl Hubenthal. Rose later contacted Hubenthal and bought the rights to the drawing for use by the team.

New Orleans Saints

New Orleans Saints
1500 Poydras Street
New Orleans, LA 70112

Team Colors: Old Gold and Black
Year Founded: 1966
Stadium: Louisiana Superdome
Seating Capacity: 71,330

THE SAINTS came marching into New Orleans, Louisiana, on November 1st, 1966—a most appropriate date since it was All Saints Day.

The National Football League awarded New Orleans the 16th franchise in history on this day. On December 15, Vic Schwenk was named president of the new team.

The team went without a nickname until January 9, 1967, when the team name was announced as the New Orleans Saints.

The Saints name was chosen by team officials because of the date the franchise was awarded to the city. It is also believed the team was named after the famous jazz song "When the Saints Come Marching In" which reflects the city's great love for their own brand of music.

Some nicknames travel well, while others don't. The Detroit Pistons' move from Fort Wayne to the auto capital of the world worked out fine. So did the Brooklyn Dodgers name when fans exchanged dodging trolleys on the east coast to dodging freeway traffic in Los Angeles.

But the Los Angeles Lakers name doesn't fit as well as in Minneapolis. The Jazz didn't fare as well in Utah as in New Orleans. With its Mormon tradition, Utah would have done better to have purchased the New Orleans Saints.

New York Giants

New York Giants
Giants Stadium
East Rutherford, NJ 07073

Team Colors: Blue, Red, and White
Year Founded: 1925
Stadium: Giants Stadium
Seating Capacity: 76,891

THE NEW YORK GIANTS, of the National Football League, were founded by Timothy J. Mara, who paid $500 for the new franchise in 1925.

Mara, an avid baseball fan, named his football team the Giants after baseball's New York Giants who played at the Polo Grounds.

The Giants name fit the team's popularity very well, During their first year, a record crowd of over 70,000 jammed the Polo Grounds to see the Giants take on Red Grange and the Chicago Bears.

The name also fit the players and their outstanding record. In 1927, they finished with an 11-1-1 record built on a tremendous defense which featured two all-time tackles who were a pair of musclemen unmatched in the league, Steve Owen and Cal Hubbard. During their 13 game season, only two rushing touchdowns were scored against the Giants.

Philadelphia Eagles

Philadelphia Eagles
Broad Street and Pattison Ave.
Philadelphia, PA 19148-5201

Team Colors: Kelly Green, Silver, and White
Year Founded: 1924—Frankford Yellowjackets
Stadium: Veterans Stadium
Seating Capacity: 71,529

THE PHILADELPHIA EAGLES team name was determined following a political campaign in the early 1930s.

Prior to this, the Frankford Yellowjackets, who played in an old section of Philadelphia called Frankford, went bankrupt. At that time, Bert Bell and Lud Wray bought the National Football League franchise for $2,500.

The Great Depression was no easy time to start a business, yet these two brave new owners took a risk. The new professional football team name Philadelphia Eagles was chosen in honor of President Franklin Roosevelt's New Deal and National Recovery Act. Both of these political campaigns had the American Eagle as their symbol.

Roosevelt intended for his "Eagle" to represent the United States industrial rebirth. By selecting Eagles as its team name, both the new owners and Philadelphia fans hoped to see their team reborn from the dismal days in Frankford.

The team eventually changed their team colors from blue and yellow to kelly green. Blue and yellow were originally chosen because they were the city of Philadelphia colors.

Hugh Brown, a football writer for the Philadelphia Bulletin, wrote the following concerning the decision to change the team colors: "Blue and yellow were abandoned because at least one of the colors (yellow) became too symbolical of the team's decadence. Bell mixed blue and yellow and somehow came up with green."

Phoenix Cardinals

Phoenix Cardinals
Tempe, AZ 85281

Team Colors: Cardinal Red, White, and Black
Year Founded: 1920—Chicago Cardinals
Stadium: Arizona State Univ. Sundome
Seating Capacity: 73,000

THE PHOENIX CARDINALS, of the National Football Conference, are recognized as the oldest continuing franchise in the National Football League.

The original Cardinal team was founded by Chris O'Brien, who first organized the team in 1898, when a group began playing on Chicago's South Side. This was the informal start of the famous Chicago Cardinals football team.

The name Cardinal was not given to the team because of the bird, but rather for the color of uniforms which O'Brien purchased for the team. He bought used maroon football jerseys from the University of Chicago for the team.

"That's not maroon, it's Cardinal Red," commented O'Brien on introducing the team uniforms—and the Cardinals it has been ever since.

The team grew in popularity and in 1920, the Chicago Cardinals became a charter member of the American Football League.

Although the Cardinals moved to St. Louis, Missouri, in 1960, the team kept the same name and uniforms. In 1988, the team moved to the Phoenix, Ariz., area after plans to build a larger football stadium in St. Louis failed to materialize.

The Cardinal logo was not adopted by the team until late in the team's history. Looking back, the actual logo for the team would not be the bird, but the original color of the uniforms used by the team in 1899.

San Francisco Forty Niners

San Francisco Forty Niners
711 Nevada Street
Redwood City, CA 94061

Team Colors: Forty Niners Gold and Scarlet
Year Founded: 1946—All-American Conference
Stadium: Candlestick Park
Seating Capacity: 61,115

THE SAN FRANCISCO 49ERS, selected their nickname based on a historical event that had hit the city almost 100 years before. The event was the 1849 California Gold Rush which made many people rich, but left many more without a dime in their pockets.

In 1946, San Francisco native and trucking company executive Tony Marabito bought an All-American Conference pro football franchise and based it in San Francisco. During the team's early days, they were often tagged by sports writers as the San Francisco Prospectors.

After experimenting with a few different names, part-owner Alan Sorrell suggested San Francisco 49ers. Sorrell felt that because there were very few pro football teams west of the Mississippi River, team owners were taking a risk establishing a team in San Francisco. He felt there was a parallel between the team officials and the gold prospectors of 1849—the 49ers, who were each taking a risk on the west coast. Thus the team name of 49ers.

When the A.A.C. folded prior to the 1950 football season, the National Football League accepted three teams from the bankrupt league. Along with San Francisco, Baltimore and Cleveland were also admitted to the NFL.

The team really felt like prospectors in professional football during their first year with only three wins and nine losses. A rival coach described them as "not big enough or tough enough" during their first NFL season—something they overcame in a big way during their second year of play with a record of seven wins, four losses and one tie.

Tampa Bay Buccaneers

Tampa Bay Buccaneers
One Buccaneer Place
Tampa, FL 33607

Team Colors: Orange, Red, and White
Year Founded: 1975
Stadium: Tampa Stadium
Seating Capacity: 72,126

WHEN TAMPA received an expansion franchise in the National Football League in 1975, the team name of Tampa Bay Buccaneers was based on the legends of the pirates who sailed off the Florida coast hundreds of years ago.

Tampa Radio Station WFLA held a contest to name the new team. Dr. Richard Molloy of Tampa won a television set and a set of tickets for the 1976 season for his winning entry of Tampa Bay Buccaneers. Other names that were considered were Sailors, Rough Riders, 76ers, and Crackers.

"It was unanimous," commented team committee chairman James M. McEwen on the new team name. "It seems to fit. We are on the water. Water people first settled in the area. Boating is a way of life and our history is rich in pirate stories. We believe it embraces the area."

Team owner Hugh F. Culverhouse added, "It catches the spirit. I think of the coast-line community and the rich history of so-called freeboaters whom they tell me took charge in their days of pirating and buccaneering. Well, we want our football team to be as aggressive, high-spirited, and colorful as were the old buccaneers. As for Tampa Bay, it laps up on the shores of most surrounding communities. I like it."

"The Pirate theme gives great opportunity for use of the imagination with symbols, costuming, and even adjectives," said McEwen. "At least we hope our Tampa Bay Bucs sack some people."

Among nicknames of the sea are Dolphins, Mariners, Seahawks, Penguins, Whalers, and Clippers.

Washington Redskins

Washington Redskins
13832 Redskin Drive
Redskin Park
P. O. Box 17247
Washington, D.C. 20041

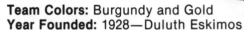

Team Colors: Burgundy and Gold
Year Founded: 1928—Duluth Eskimos
Stadium: Robert F. Kennedy Memorial Stadium
Seating Capacity: 55,031

THE WASHINGTON REDSKINS, one of the premier football franchises in the National Football League, originated in Boston, Massachusetts, after moving from Duluth, Minnesota.

The Duluth Eskimos were pro football's traveling show in the late 1920s and early 1930s. No opposing teams wanted to play in Duluth because it was too cold, too small, and they could not make enough money.

So the Eskimos team traveled. One year they played 26 games—all on the road. But it couldn't last because times were changing, the football league was growing and train bills were becoming astronomical.

In 1932, George P. Marshall headed a syndicate to buy the Eskimos and supply Boston with a National Football League team. The partners were granted permission to play at the Boston Braves baseball field and the new NFL team donned the name Boston Braves.

One year later, the Boston football team moved to Fenway Park—the home of the Boston Red Sox of the American League in baseball. To improve business relations with their new landlord, the football team disposed of the Braves nickname and named themselves Redskins after the team to whom they were now writing their rent checks.

Just five years later, an even bigger change was made in the professional football team's operation. On February 13, 1937, the Washington Redskins were officially born in the nation's capitol—thanks to local sponsors that transferred the team from Boston to Washington D.C.

The famed Redskins Band was also founded the same year. This team band was the first of its kind in the NFL and led to many other bands formed for entertainment purposes in football stadiums around the league.

Eastern Division

National Basketball Association

Atlanta Hawks

Atlanta Hawks
100 Techwood Dr. NW
Atlanta, GA 30303

Team Colors: Red, White, and Gold
Year Founded: 1948—Tri-Cities Blackhawks
Arena: The Omni
Seating Capacity: 16,074

UNLIKE MOST professional sports teams, Atlanta Hawks officials didn't have the slightest idea where their team's nickname came from. And it's understandable since the team played in three cities over a 20-year period before settling in Atlanta.

Like the Chicago Blackhawks of the National Hockey League, the Tri-Cities Blackhawks of the National Basketball Association were named after the famous Sauk Indian Chief Black Hawk.

The tri-cities, which include Moline and Rock Island, Illinois; and

Davenport, Iowa; were granted an NBA franchise in 1948. Since Chief Black Hawk's tribe was located in Rock Island and because a major part of the 1831 Black Hawk War was fought in the surrounding areas, the team was naturally named Tri-Cities Blackhawks.

However, in 1951, the team migrated north to Milwaukee where a shortened version of the name was used. The team became known as the Milwaukee Hawks.

But only four years later the team moved once again. Starting their continual journey south, they moved back along the banks of the Mississippi River where they set up camp in St. Louis, Missouri. The move did not affect their name as the team was called the St. Louis Hawks.

After 13 good seasons in St. Louis, the team moved further south again to Atlanta in 1968, just in time to win the division championship. The team still kept the Hawk name and the team has been the Atlanta Hawks ever since.

Upon writing to Hawks Public Relations Assistant Scott Wiggins on the origin of the Hawk name, he replied, "Beyond knowing that the Atlanta Hawks originated from the St. Louis Hawks, I am unable to provide you with any further information regarding the name. Most of the team's records and general information about the club and its origin are not available prior to their arrival in Atlanta."

Apparently, the Atlanta Hawks organization did not know exactly where their name originated. And after playing professional basketball in four different cities in 20 years, who could possibly blame them?

Boston Celtics

Boston Celtics
150 Causeway Street
Boston, MA 02114

Team Colors: Green and White
Year Founded: 1946
Arena: Boston Garden
Seating Capacity: 15,320

ON JUNE 6, 1946, a group of national arena owners met in New York to discuss forming a basketball association that could fill the arenas with paying customers between boxing matches and hockey games.

Thus the Basketball Association of America was formed (which later merged with the National Basketball League to form the National Basketball Association) and the Boston Celtics, one of the original teams, has been around ever since.

The name Celtics was associated with the basketball team known as the "Original Celtics" founded in the 1920's by Jim Furey. This team was one of the first truly successful pro basketball teams and helped bring about the formation of organized professional basketball.

During the summer of 1946, the team name was determined. In a conversation with publicist J. Howard McHugh, team founder Walter Brown stated, "Wait, I've got it—the Celtics. We'll call them the Boston Celtics! The name has a great basketball tradition. And Boston is full of Irishmen. Yes, that's it. We'll put them in green uniforms and call them the Boston Celtics."

Yet the Celtics did not immediately have much luck o' the Irish. In their first home game on November 5, 1946, a two-handed set shot by Kevin (Chuck) Connors—who would later become a famous sharpshooter on TV's "The Rifleman," shattered the glass backboard. The game was delayed over an hour—before it finally got underway again.

The Celtics had attendance problems that year. The top home crowd of 6,327 didn't even half fill the Boston Arena. The team finished in last place for the 1946-1947 season with only 22 wins against 38 losses. The team was so bad that they were often referred to as the "Boston Smeltics."

Yet things picked up for the team as they were able to make the playoffs the following year. This was the start of the fantastic winning tradition that the Celtics are known for today.

Chicago Bulls

Chicago Bulls
One Magnificent Mile
980 N. Michigan Ave.
Suite 1600
Chicago, IL 60611

Team Colors: Red, White, and Black
Year Founded: 1966
Arena: Chicago Stadium
Seating Capacity: 17,374

THE NICKNAME of the Chicago's representative in the National Basketball Association originated with the team's first owner, Richard Klein.

Klein, who founded the club in 1966, decided to name the team the Chicago Bulls. The reasoning behind his decision was that the fighting bull, as known from centuries of bull ring history, had a relentless fighting attitude along with the instinct to never say quit.

Both of the above qualities are very necessary for a championship club and Klein hoped his Chicago athletes would live up to the team name.

Cleveland Cavaliers

Cleveland Cavaliers
The Coliseum
P.O. Box 355
Richfield, OH 44286

Team Colors: Burnt Orange, White,, and Royal Blue
Year Founded: 1970
Arena: Richfield Coliseum
Seating Capacity: 20,900

WHEN CLEVELAND received a National Basketball Association franchise prior to the 1970 season, the team owner turned the decision on the team nickname over to the fans. Out of all the entries submitted to the local newspapers, the name of Cleveland Cavaliers was selected as the new team name.

Following the contest, the logo of a 17th century Englishman sporting a long sabre was created for use by the team.

In the spring of 1983, the Cavaliers were sold to George and Gordon Gund. In an attempt to form a new image, (and hopefully get off the losing track), the team colors were changed from wine and gold to orange, white, and blue. Also, the club adopted another logo which featured "Cavs" in capital letters with the "v" as a basketball goal and net.

Detroit Pistons

Detroit Pistons
Pontiac Silverdome
1200 Featherstone
Pontiac, MI 48507

Team Colors: Red, White, and Blue
Year Founded: 1948—Fort Wayne Zollner Pistons
Arena: The Palace of Auburn Hills
Seating Capacity: 21,525

THE DETROIT PISTONS of the National Basketball Association originated in Fort Wayne, Indiana, under the name of Fort Wayne Zollner Pistons. Team owner Fred Zollner uniquely named his club after himself and his business that enabled him to purchase a franchise—a piston manufacturing company located in Fort Wayne.

However, Zollner decided to move his team to a bigger market. And in 1957, Zollner and the Pistons moved to Detroit.

The name remained the same—and fit right in with the Motor City's reputation as the auto capital of the world. *(The Detroit Pistons will soon move into a 20,000 seat arena in Auburn Hills, Mich.)*

Indiana Pacers

Indiana Pacers
Two W. Washington
Suite 510
Indianapolis, IN 46204

Team Colors: Gold and Blue
Year Founded: 1967—American Basketball Association
Arena: Market Square Arena
Seating Capacity: 16,912

THE INDIANA PACERS of the National Basketball Association selected their team nickname in a different way from most other teams. Their selection of a name was determined by what they wished to accomplish in the new league.

On June 16, 1967, during a press conference for the new American Basketball Association franchise, it was announced the team would be named the Indiana Pacers. Team officials decided upon the nickname because the organization intended to set the "pace" in professional basketball.

Although the Pacers became part of the National Basketball Association in 1976, along with New Jersey, San Antonio, and Denver, the team remained under the same name and logo it had used for 9 years.

Milwaukee Bucks

Milwaukee Bucks
901 North Fourth Street
Milwaukee, WI 53203

Team Colors: Forest Green, Red and White
Year Founded: 1968
Arena: Bradley Center
Seating Capacity: 19,000

ON MAY 22, 1968, the Milwaukee basketball organization finally got a name—the Milwaukee Bucks. The name was chosen from about 14,000 contest entries and the winner was R. D. Treblicox of Whitefish Bay, Wisconsin. He won a new automobile for his winning suggestion.

The reasoning behind the team officials selection of the Bucks name was that it fits the wildlife atmosphere of Wisconsin, fits the sport of basketball, easily adapts to promotional use, is a unique name among professional teams, and as Treblicox stated, "Bucks are spirited, good jumpers, fast and agile. These are exceptional qualities for basketball players."

Other suggested names were: Skunks, Beavers, Stags, Hornets, Stallions, Ponies, Badgers, Packers and Braves. Many Indian tribe names were also entered.

Evidently, the judges were most interested in names that described the fish and game area, "because it is indigenous to Wisconsin," stated general manager John Erickson. "The predominance of bucks led us to that."

New Jersey Nets

New Jersey Nets
Brendan Byrne Arena
185 E. Union Avenue
East Rutherford, NJ 07073

Team Colors: Red, White, and Blue
Year Founded: 1967—New Jersey Americans (A.B.A.)
Arena: Brendan Byrne Arena
Seating Capacity: 20,149

WHEN NEW JERSEY entered the American Basketball Association with their New Jersey Americans in 1967, little did the fans know how short a period of time they would have to cheer for the team. By the following season, the team would be playing in New York.

Yet 10 years later, the team would again return to the Garden State.

During the Americans first season, the team did well enough to qualify for the last playoff spot by tying with the Kentucky Colonels. The Americans, unable to play on their home floor at Teaneck Armory because of a previously-scheduled circus and with the optional floor at Commack Arena in Long Island found "unplayable," were forced to forfeit the tiebreaker game with the Colonels.

During the summer of 1968, the franchise moved to Commack, Long Island, and was renamed the New York Nets after one of the most important parts of the basketball game—the net.

After winning the last A.B.A. championship, the New York Nets, along with Spurs, Nuggets, and Pacers, joined the National Basketball Association. Yet prior to the 1977-78 season, the team was moved once again to New Jersey. However, the name stayed with the team as they were now known as the New Jersey Nets.

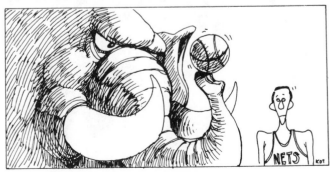

New York Knicks

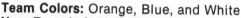

New York Knicks
Madison Square Garden Center
Four Pennsylvania Plaza
New York, NY 10001

Team Colors: Orange, Blue, and White
Year Founded: 1946—New York Knickerbockers
Arena: Madison Square Garden
Seating Capacity: 19,591

NED IRISH, who played the main role in bringing a National Basketball Association franchise to New York in 1946, is perhaps the only one who knows exactly how the team name of New York Knickerbockers originated. Irish, who is long since dead, took most of the team's historical file data with him.

No minutes of the team formation meetings or information pertaining to the organization of the franchise can be found in any team files or in the New York newspapers.

However, when the question of the origin of the name came up a few years ago, the concensus among management was that the Knickerbocker name emanated from the old Dutch settlement in New York and the Knickers—long trousers banded at the knee—which menfolk wore during this time.

Although this explanation may not be totally accurate, team officials accept this theory as how the name originated.

Philadelphia 76ers

Philadelphia 76ers
P.O. Box 25040
Philadelphia, PA 19147

Team Colors: Red, White, and Blue
Year Founded: 1949—Syracuse Nationals
Arena: The Spectrum
Seating Capacity: 18,276

AFTER PHILADELPHIA lost the Warriors when the team transferred to San Francisco in 1962, two men, Irv Kosloff and Ike Richman, went shopping to bring a professional basketball team back to the city.

In the spring of 1963, Kosloff and Richman teamed together to purchase the Syracuse Nats and Philadelphia once again had a National Basketball Association team.

The team was renamed the Philadelphia 76ers in honor of the signing of the United States Declaration of Independence July 4, 1776, by the Continental Congress at Independence Hall, located in Philadelphia.

Washington Bullets

Washington Bullets
Capital Centre
One Harry S. Truman Drive
Landover, MD 20785

Team Colors: Red, White, and Blue
Year Founded: 1961—Chicago Packers
Arena: Capital Centre
Seating Capacity: 19,105

THE CURRENT WASHINGTON BULLETS of the National Basketball Association were named after the original basketball team located in Baltimore.

When Baltimore was first given a basketball franchise in 1946, the team was named after a nearby foundry that produced ammunition for U.S. soldiers during World War II. As you would guess, the team was named the Baltimore Bullets. However, the team disbanded a few years later.

The current Washington franchise joined the NBA in 1961 as the Chicago Packers. Owner David Trager named the club after his packing company. But only one year later the team name was changed to Chicago Zephyrs.

The team moved to Baltimore in 1963 and was renamed Baltimore Bullets after the city's original team.

The Bullets remained in Baltimore until 1973 when the team jumped to Washington, D.C., and was named the Capitol Bullets. However, the team name did not fit well with the club and in 1974 the team was named Washington Bullets and has remained the same ever since.

Western Division

National Basketball Association

Dallas Mavericks

Dallas Mavericks
Reunion Arena
777 Sports Street
Dallas, TX 75207

Team Colors: Blue and Green
Year Founded: 1980
Arena: Reunion Arena
Seating Capacity: 17,007

DALLAS, TEXAS, tried to get a National Basketball franchise as early as 1978. That's when Dallas Mayor Robert Folsom and pro basketball executive Norm Sonju looked into purchasing the Buffalo Braves and moving them to the "Big D."

The Braves moved to San Diego, however, and became the Clippers, thus ruling out the possibility of Dallas landing a franchise.

Sonju was named general manager of the proposed Dallas franchise in 1979. His full-time job was to obtain a basketball team for Dallas.

With hard work and determination by Sonju, Dallas was given permission to obtain a NBA expansion team on September 27, 1979.

A fan contest by WBAP radio was held to name the new basketball team. The name Dallas Mavericks was announced on May 1, 1980, after being selected by the club's executive committee. The name Mavericks was chosen because of its tie-in with the world famous cowboy image of Texas.

The team was built on an NBA dispersal draft—in which every NBA team had to sacrifice one player from their current roster for the new Dallas expansion team.

Denver Nuggets

Denver Nuggets
P. O. Box 4658
Denver, CO 80204-0658

Team Colors: White, Blue, Green, Yellow, Red,
Purple, and Orange
Year Founded: 1967—Denver Rockets (A.B.A.)
Arena: McNichols Sports Arena
Seating Capacity: 17,251

THE CURRENT NAME of the Denver Nuggets of the National Basketball Association was selected because another professional basketball franchise was already using the team's original Rockets name.

When Denver played its first season in the American Basketball Association in 1967, the team was known as the Denver Rockets. Before the 1974 season, the team was sold and the new owners had plans for the Rockets to join the NBA. However, the Houston Rockets were using the same name. Therefore, Denver team officials decided to rename the club.

The team name of Denver Nuggets was picked as the new nickname. Nuggets refers to the 19th century period in Colorado when people rushed to the area when gold and silver mining were booming. The mining rush helped make Denver the prospering city that it is today.

However, the Nuggets nickname was not really new. The original Denver Nuggets team was a charter member of the NBA, but folded after only one year of existence.

There are several religious nicknames, including Saints, Angels, and Padres.

Golden State Warriors

Golden State Warriors
Oakland Coliseum Arena
Oakland, CA 94621-1995

Team Colors: Gold and Blue
Year Founded: 1946—Philadelphia Warriors
Arena: Oakland Coliseum Arena
Seating Capacity: 13,237

WHEN PHILADELPHIA became a charter member of the National Basketball Association in 1946, one of the first tasks of the team officials was to name the new club. It was decided to name the team after the original Philadelphia basketball team—the Warriors who began play in the American Basketball League in 1925 under coach Eddie Baker.

After 17 seasons in Philadelphia, the team bounced all the way to the other side of the United States and settled in San Francisco. The team kept the same name and was called the San Francisco Warriors.

But once again the team found themselves moving. This time, however, it was just a short jump across San Francisco Bay as the team made their new home in Oakland in 1971.

In an attempt to get the whole state of California involved with the team, team officials named the club the Golden State Warriors upon their arrival.

Houston Rockets

Houston Rockets
10 Greenway Plaza
Houston, TX 77046

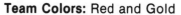

Team Colors: Red and Gold
Year Founded: 1967—San Diego Rockets
Arena: The Summit
Seating Capacity: 15,676

ON JANUARY 11, 1967, San Diego became the 12th member of the National Basketball Association. To select a name for their new NBA club, the basketball fans of San Diego were asked to choose a nickname for the team.

Out of 10,000 entries, more than 1,000 different names were submitted. After careful deliberation, a group of leading citizens chose Rockets because it fit in with San Diego's theme of a "City in Motion" while reflecting the outstanding growth of space-age industries in San Diego.

After the 1970-71 season, the San Diego Rockets moved to Houston, Texas, and became the Houston Rockets. The Rockets name is still a valid name today because the NASA space program is located in Houston.

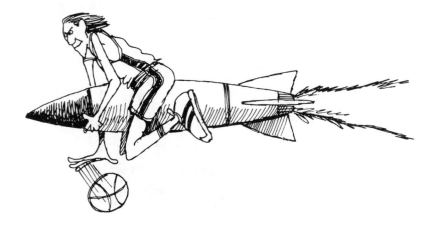

Los Angeles Clippers

Los Angeles Clippers
3939 South Figueroa St.
Los Angeles, CA 90037-1292

Team Colors: Red, White, and Blue
Year Founded: 1970—Buffalo Braves
Arena: Los Angeles Sports Arena
Seating Capacity: 15,371

AFTER LOSING the Rockets to Houston in 1971, San Diego went without a National Basketball Association team until 1978, when the Buffalo Braves moved to California.

Upon reaching San Diego, team officials thought the name "Braves" did not fit in with San Diego's image. A contest was held to name the team and the entry of San Diego Clippers was selected as the winner.

The reason that Clippers was selected as the new team name was the fact that San Diego was known for the great sailing ships—"clippers"—that passed through the San Diego harbor many years ago.

Although the franchise moved to Los Angeles in 1984, the team name survived as the team is now known as the Los Angeles Clippers.

Los Angeles Lakers

Los Angeles Lakers
The Forum
P. O. Box 10
Inglewood, CA 90306

Team Colors: Royal Purple and Gold
Year Founded: 1948—Minneapolis Lakers
Arena: Los Angeles Forum
Seating Capacity: 17,505

WHEN MINNEAPOLIS was granted a National Basketball Association franchise prior to the 1948 season, team officials named the club the Minneapolis Lakers. The name was based on the thousands of lakes in the state and the state motto "The Land of 10,000 Lakes." The team went on to win the league championship in their inaugural season.

When the team moved to Los Angeles prior to the 1960 season, they brought the team name of Lakers with them. It was ironic that the team became known as the Los Angeles Lakers because of the fact that there are few, if any, lakes in the Los Angeles area.

In 1985, a Salt Lake City news columnist proposed that Los Angeles and Utah trade nicknames that would better suit each of the NBA teams. He suggested that the nickname "Lakers" would more appropriately represent Salt Lake City, and "Jazz" would be more natural with the city of Los Angeles.

Phoenix Suns

Phoenix Suns
2910 N. Central Ave.
Phoenix, AZ 85012

Team Colors: Purple, Orange, and Copper
Year Founded: 1968
Arena: Veterans Memorial Coliseum
Seating Capacity: 14,519

WHEN CO-OWNER Karl Eller was stumped with the task of naming the new National Basketball franchise in Phoenix, he asked the board of directors, "Why not throw it open to the fans and see what they come up with?"

Team officials had first shunned the idea of a "Name the Team Contest" and promised they would have a team name after one week. Apparently, they could not find an appropriate name and announced a public contest.

As an incentive to draw thousands of participants, the club announced that everyone entering would receive a free ticket to a future basketball game. Team officials also said that the contest winner would receive $1,000 in cash, two season tickets, and a one-year membership to the Stadium Club.

Out of over 28,000 suggestions and 465 different names, team officials chose Phoenix Suns as the official team nickname, which is a parallel with Arizona's year-round sunshine and tropical climate. Other names in the running were Dust Devils, Suntanos, Dudes, Wrens, Tumbleweeds, Sunspots, Gems, Scorpions, and Rattlers.

Portland Trail Blazers

Portland Trail Blazers
700 NE Multnomah Street
Portland, OR 97232-2172

Team Colors: Scarlet, Black, and White
Year Founded: 1970
Arena: Portland Memorial Coliseum
Seating Capacity: 12,666

WHEN HARRY GLICKMAN founded Portland's entry to the National Basketball Association in 1970, one of his goals was to develop an original nickname. He wanted a name that was not associated with any colleges in Oregon and had not been used by anyone else in the state.

Team officials held a "Name the Team" contest which drew over 10,000 entries. The nickname of Portland Trail Blazers, submitted by 172 contestants, was selected by the committee as the most suitable for the club. The new name was announced at the Seattle-New York game in Portland in 1970.

"We are delighted," stated Glickman. "We feel that Trail Blazers reflects both the ruggedness of the Pacific Northwest and the start of a major league era in our state."

Sacramento Kings

Sacramento Kings
1515 Sports Drive
Sacramento, CA 95834

Team Colors: Red, White, and Blue
Year Founded: 1948—Rochester Royals
Arena: Arco Arena
Seating Capacity: 10,333

THE SACRAMENTO KINGS of the National Basketball Association began as the Rochester Royals in 1948. After nine seasons in Rochester, the club was moved to Cincinnati and renamed the Cincinnati Royals.

In 1972, the team was moved to Kansas City, Missouri, and named the Kansas City-Omaha Kings after the public voted on the team name. Other nicknames considered were the Steers, River Kings, Tornadoes, Plainsmen, Barons, Regals, Scouts, Crowns, and Stars.

"I'm very satisfied with the name Kings," commented team general manager Joe Axelson. "I'm also very happy with the reception we have received in both cities.

"We are sorry to give up the Royal's name, but we did it to accommodate the Kansas City and Omaha Royals baseball teams. We felt it would eliminate confusion for the media and public alike."

In 1975, "Omaha" was dropped from the team's title and the new name of the club was Kansas City Kings.

Though the franchise moved to Sacramento, California, in 1985, the name Kings remained with the team.

San Antonio Spurs

San Antonio Spurs
HemisFair Arena
P.O. Box 530
San Antonio, TX 78292

Team Colors: Metallic Silver and Black
Year Founded: 1967—Dallas Chaparrals (A.B.A.)
Arena: HemisFair Arena
Seating Capacity: 15,800

AFTER THE American Basketball Association granted Dallas a franchise in 1967, the new club was named the Dallas Chaparrals—a name representing the famous thickets and trees located in Texas and Mexico.

However, in 1970 the name was changed to Texas Chaparrals, perhaps in an effort to get the whole state of Texas interested in the club. Yet only one year later, the club's name was returned to the city of Dallas.

In the summer of 1973, the Chaparrals moved to San Antonio. Team officials no longer felt the original name to be fitting with San Antonio's image, and sponsored a public contest to name the city's new basketball team.

After hundreds of suggestions were considered, the name of San Antonio Spurs was selected. The reasoning behind the new name was that it represented the western heritage of Texas, a crisp, professional-looking logo could be easily adopted, and the "Spurs" name was short enough for extensive use by the media.

Seattle Supersonics

Seattle Supersonics
P.O. Box 900911
Seattle, WA 98109-9711

SEATTLE SUPERSONICS
®

Team Colors: Green and Yellow
Year Founded: 1967
Arena: Seattle Kingdome
Seating Capacity: 40,192

THE SEATTLE SUPERSONICS, a 1967 National Basketball Association expansion team, selected their team name like most other professional sports teams—through a contest.

Howard E. Schmidt, of Seattle won a trip to Palm Springs, California, and season tickets for the 67-68 basketball season for his winning entry of Supersonics.

The name Supersonics was chosen from among 25,000 names because of the huge Boeing plant located in the Seattle area. During the late 1960s, Boeing, which is one of the leading manufacturers of airplanes in the United States, had proposed the building of a Concorde-style airplane. The new plane was to be known as the "Supersonic Transport."

Although the new plane idea "never got off the ground," Boeing's involvement with the city had a great effect among the public as almost 200 suggestions using the name "Sonics" were entered.

"We think the name best expresses Seattle's people, its present, and future," commented team General Manager Don Richman on the new team name.

Utah Jazz

Utah Jazz
5 Triad Center
Suite 500
Salt Lake City, UT 84180

Team Colors: Purple, Green, and Gold
Year Founded: 1974—New Orleans Jazz
Arena: The Salt Palace
Seating Capacity: 12,143

THE UTAH JAZZ professional basketball team, formerly known as the New Orleans Jazz, was named after New Orleans' great love for the predominant style of jazz music.

With its annual Mardi Gras celebration, along with the year-long partying on Bourbon Street, the city has a tremendous reputation for enjoying itself.

When New Orleans was granted a National Basketball Association in 1974, club officials chose the name Jazz to represent the city for its reputation as the internationally known "jazz capital of the world."

Although the team moved to Salt Lake City in 1979, the team kept the nickname, uniforms, colors and are now known as the Utah Jazz.

The Newest Teams In The
National Basketball Association

Unlike the other 23 NBA teams, these four newest teams will follow a four-year rotation during which each team will play in each of the various four subdivisions of the NBA. The Miami Heat and the Charlotte Hornets began playing in October 1988; the Minnesota Timberwolves and the Orlando Magic begin playing in October 1989.

Charlotte Hornets

Charlotte Hornets
2 First Union Center
Suite 2600
Charlotte, NC 28282

Mascot

Team Colors: Teal, Purple, Orange, and White
Year Founded: 1988
Arena: Charlotte Coliseum
Seating Capacity: 23,000

THE CHARLOTTE BASKETBALL club originally named their new team before they were ever awarded a franchise by the National Basketball Association.

Prior to the NBA's 1987 expansion movement, club officials formed a committee to name the team. From this committee, the nickname Charlotte Spirit was selected.

However, this brand new name never made it to the uniform manufacturer. Because public response to the name was poor, the owners gave in and held a contest once it was officially announced that an NBA team would be playing in Charlotte.

Fans submitted many names to the contest, held in conjunction with the Charlotte *Observer*. After carefully evaluating all entries, the owners selected six names and asked the public to vote on them.

Included in this group were the Gold, because legend states that gold was discovered in Charlotte even before the California rush; the Knights, because Charlotte is known as the "Queen City"; the Spirit, the owners' previous choice and the Hornets. Team officials can no longer recall what the two other possible names were.

The Hornets prevailed by a landslide vote over the other five names listed on the ballot, according to the *Observer*.

The name "Hornets" goes all the way back to the Revolutionary War when British General Charles Cornwallis wrote to the King of England in his battle report from the Carolinas that "this place is like fighting in a hornet's nest."

Actually, the Hornets is not a new name to Charlotte. Earlier there was a farm team of the Minnesota Twins in Charlotte called the Hornets, as well as a franchise in the World Football League by the same name.

Miami Heat

Miami Heat
100 Chopin Plaza
Suite 200
Miami, FL 33131

Team Colors: Orange, Red, Yellow, and Black
Year Founded: 1988
Arena: Miami Arena
Seating Capacity: 15,361

AFTER MIAMI was granted a National Basketball Association team in 1987, team officials immediately started the task of naming the club.

In an effort to get all of southern Florida involved, a "Name the Team" contest was held, and more than 5,000 entries were received. Among the names submitted were Sharks, Barracudas, Flamingos, Palm Trees, Beaches, Heat, Suntan, Shade, Tornadoes, Floridians—and a few fans even tried to clone Miami's football team—the Dolphins.

After looking over all the entries, the owners decided on the Miami Heat for the simple reason that they liked it the best.

"The Heat was it," said general partner Zev Bufman. "The owners just felt it represented the area. I like it. We're Miami. When you think of Miami, that's what you think of."

After naming the club, team officials held another contest to create a logo. After receiving 1,000 artistic entries, the choice was narrowed down to 12 logos; fans were asked to vote for one of the dozen, which were shown in the Miami *Herald* and Miami *News*. The final decision was a red-hot, flaming basketball flying through a basketball rim.

Minnesota Timberwolves

Minnesota Timberwolves
5525 Cedar Lake Road
Minneapolis, MN 55416

Team Colors: Royal Blue, Kelly Green, and Silver
Year Founded: 1989
Arena: Hubert H. Humphrey Metrodome
Seating Capacity: 17,500

THE MINNESOTA TIMBERWOLVES decided on their team name mainly because of its uniqueness.

When the organization was formed on April 22, 1987, the club sponsored a contest for area sports fans to name their new team. After officials went through 6,000 entries, the decision was narrowed down to Timberwolves and Polars.

In order to get potential fans deeply involved, public forums were held by city councils all over Minnesota. The name Timberwolves triumphed by a two-to-one margin over Polars.

Team officials like the name Timberwolves for three reasons: First, it is indigenous to Minnesota; besides Alaska, Minnesota is the only state with a significant number of this breed of wolves. Second, the name is unique; no professional sports team has ever used the name and only a few high schools (including Ely High School in northern Minnesota) have it. And, third, the name is very marketable and easy to develop a logo for.

It was decided to call the team the Minnesota Timberwolves because the team involves not only the Twin Cities but the whole Midwest, since the closest NBA teams are located in Milwaukee, Chicago, and Denver.

Orlando Magic

Orlando Magic
P.O. Box 76
Orlando, FL 32802

Team Colors: Blue, Black, and Silver
Year Founded: 1989
Arena: Orlando Arena
Seating Capacity: 15,000

THE ORLANDO professional basketball team came up with their nickname based on the great tourist attractions located in this area of Florida.

Team officials sponsored a contest with the Orlando *Sentinel* so fans could send in their suggestions for the team's new nickname. Through the newspaper contest, names were narrowed down to two—Magic and Juice.

Some fans wanted to use "sleight of hand" and have the Magic name selected. Other fans wanted to put the "squeeze" on club owners and have Juice named as the winner, since it ties in perfectly with the area's orange and grapefruit groves. These two names were sent to a panel of local community leaders who selected Magic as the winner. Did they work hard at picking a winner or did they simply pull the name Magic out of a hat?

"Magic is synonymous with this area," said the team's general manager Pat Williams. "We are the tourist capital of the world. We have the Magic Kingdom and Disney World. The tourism slogan is 'Come to the Magic'."

Undoubtedly, the Magic's top brass hopes to pull some tricks on their NBA opponents in the future.

Clarence Campbell Conference
National Hockey League

Calgary Flames

Calgary Flames
P.O. Box 1540 Station "M"
Calgary, Alberta T2P 3B9

Team Colors: Orange, Red, and White
Year Founded: 1972—Atlanta Flames
Arena: Olympic Saddledome
Seating Capacity: 16,762

AS SOMEONE once said, "There is a lot more that comes out of the South than just cotton." For the people of Alberta, truer words were never spoken.

The history of the Flames organization began when a group of Georgia businessmen, headed by Tom Cousins, started their search for a National Hockey League team to play in Atlanta.

Based on solid marketing research, the existence of the Atlanta Hawks of the NBA which had moved from St. Louis just four years earlier, and the completion of the modern Omni Arena, Cousins was officially granted an NHL franchise on June 6, 1972.

After receiving the franchise, team officials sponsored a contest to name the new club. With the Atlanta media serving as judges, the contest attracted over 10,000 entries. When the winning entry of Atlanta Flames was announced, the club had a name.

The team was named after a historical incident in the Civil War in which General Sherman captured the city of Atlanta and burned down the city. The flames that swallowed the city were eventually extinguished and the rebirth of the capital of Georgia began.

However, on May 21, 1980, Nelson Skalbania and a group of Alberta businessmen purchased the Atlanta franchise and moved the team to Calgary. The Flames would no longer skate with the fiery "A," but would now sport the explosive-looking "C."

Chicago Blackhawks

Chicago Blackhawks
1800 W. Madison Street
Chicago, IL 60612

Team Colors: Black, Red, and White
Year Founded: 1926
Arena: Chicago Stadium
Seating Capacity: 17,100

THE CHICAGO BLACKHAWKS of the National Hockey League were named after the fighting unit in which the team's original owner served during the first World War.

Major Frederic McLaughlin, who purchased the team in 1926, was a World War I veteran who served in an artillery unit named the Black Hawk Division. The division was named after the great chief of the Sauk Indians who roamed the midwest in the 1800s.

Chief Black Hawk led the Sauks in a two year battle against the Illinois State Militia over land disagreements in the Black Hawk War of 1831.

Now Chief Black Hawk rides proudly on every jersey. The team logo symbolizes the aggressiveness and determination of the Sauk tribe which has led the team to many Stanley Cup playoffs.

Cowboy and Indian names include Braves, Redskins, Indians, Chiefs, Blackhawks, Hawks, Cowboys, Spurs, and Rangers.

Detroit Red Wings

Detroit Red Wings
600 Civic Center Drive
Detroit, MI 48226

Team Colors: Red and White
Year Founded: 1926—Detroit Cougars
Arena: Joe Louis Sports Arena
Seating Capacity: 19,275

THE STORY of professional hockey in Detroit began on September 25, 1926, when a group of local businessmen purchased a National Hockey League franchise and brought in the Victoria Cougars of the Western Hockey League to Detroit.

On arrival of the team in Detroit, team officials chose to have the team remain the Cougars. The team finished in last place during their first season in the Motor City.

In 1930, the team changed its name to Falcons to try to bring some luck to the hockey team. Yet the team again failed to finish above .500.

During the summer of 1932, the club was purchased by industrialist James Norris, and the team was renamed once again—this time becoming the Red Wings.

The name was imported from Canada, where Norris had earlier played on a team called the Winged Wheelers which was part of the Montreal Athletic Association. The team's logo, a winged wheel, struck Norris as a natural for his new team, which was representing the Motor City.

Edmonton Oilers

Edmonton Oilers
Northlands Coliseum
Edmonton, Alberta T5B 4M9

Team Colors: Blue and Orange
Year Founded: 1972—Alberta Oilers (W.H.A.)
Arena: Northlands Coliseum
Seating Capacity: 17,490

WHEN EDMONTON, ALBERTA, was granted a World Hockey Association franchise in 1972, a contest was held to name the new club.

The name Alberta Oilers was selected out of thousands of entries. The name was chosen because Edmonton is situated in the region that produces the most oil in all of Canada. Ever since a large oil discovery was made 15 miles south of Edmonton in 1949, much of the growth of the province of Alberta has been centered around the oil industry.

The name was changed to Edmonton Oilers prior to the club's second season, shading away from provincial names.

The Oilers entered the National Hockey League in 1979, and the team name and logo have remained the same.

Los Angeles Kings

Los Angeles Kings
The Forum
P. O. Box 10
Inglewood, CA 90306

Team Colors: Gold and Purple
Year Founded: 1967
Arena: Los Angeles Forum
Seating Capacity: 16,005

SELECTING THE NICKNAME for the Los Angeles entry in the National Hockey League took the same course as many other professional sports teams. There was a contest among fans held prior to the start of the 1967 hockey season and the winning Kings name was selected by franchise owner Jack Kent Cooke.

Cooke was no newcomer to professional sports, having also owned the Los Angeles Lakers of the National Basketball League and The Forum where both teams played their games. Cooke sold both teams and the arena to Jerry Buss in 1979 for $67.5 million, the largest sports transaction in history at that time.

With the team often known by the slogan, "Worth Their Weight in Gold," this may account for the selection of gold and purple as the Kings official team colors.

Minnesota North Stars

Minnesota North Stars
Metropolitan Center
Bloomington, MN 55420-1693

Team Colors: Green and Yellow
Year Founded: 1967
Arena: Metropolitan Sports Center
Seating Capacity: 15,184

THE MINNESOTA NORTH STARS, prior to their 1967-68 initial season in the National Hockey League, held a contest among fans in the Minnesota and St. Paul area to determine a name for the new hockey club.

This was not unusual for naming a new professional sports team as similar contests have been held by a number of other professional sports teams around the country.

Since the Minnesota state nickname is "Etoile du Nord," or "Star of the North," it was only fitting that the team be called the Minnesota North Stars.

Actually, the North Stars name was submitted by a number of sports fans in the nickname contest and was the easy choice of team organizers.

St. Louis Blues

St. Louis Blues
5700 Oakland Ave.
St. Louis, MO 63110

Team Colors: Blue and Yellow
Year Founded: 1967
Arena: St. Louis Arena
Seating Capacity: 17,740

WHEN ST. LOUIS was awarded a National Hockey League franchise as six new expansion teams entered the league, owner Sid Salomon, Jr. began thinking of a name for his team.

After dissatisfaction with the suggested names of Apollo and Mercury, Salomon decided on St. Louis Blues.

"The name of the team has to be Blues. It's part of the city where W. C. Handy composed his famed song while thinking of his girl one morning," commented Salomon after the famous song "St. Louis Blues."

"No matter where you go in this town there's singing," said Salomon. "It's the spirit of St. Louis."

Toronto Maple Leafs

Toronto Maple Leafs
60 Carlton Street
Toronto, Canada M5B 1L1

Team Colors: Royal Blue and White
Year Founded: 1917—Toronto Arenas
Arena: Maple Leaf Gardens
Seating Capacity: 16,485

THE TORONTO MAPLE LEAFS, of the National Hockey League, originated as the Toronto Arenas—who began play in 1917. The team was obviously named after their home court, which was known as the old Mutual Street Arena.

Prior to the 1919 season, however, Toronto ownership renamed the club the Toronto St. Patricks. Yet the St. Patricks name would only last seven seasons in Toronto.

On Valentine's Day, 1927, Conn Smythe bought the St. Patricks and renamed the team the Toronto Maple Leafs. The club was named after the Maple Leaf Regiment—a famous Canadian fighting unit in World War I.

The name also fits in ideally with the surrounding community of Toronto, which is the capital of Ontario. Of all of Ontario, one-half of the land is covered by vast forests—many of which are the towering maple trees.

Vancouver Canucks

Vancouver Canucks
100 North Renfrew Street
Vancouver, British Columbia V5K 3N7

Team Colors: Gold, Orange, Black, and White
Year Founded: 1970
Arena: Pacific Coliseum
Seating Capacity: 15,613

THE VANCOUVER CANUCKS, a National Hockey League expansion team, received their team nickname after a legendary Canadian logger.

As the legend states, Johnny Canuck was a great logger who was also an excellent skater and hockey player in his spare time.

As the term "Yankee" is often used to refer to Americans, "Canuck" is also a slang term for a Canadian.

Although the NHL ignored Vancouver's request for a team for some time, the city was granted a franchise in 1970. Thus were born the Vancouver Canucks.

Winnipeg Jets

Winnipeg Jets
15-1430 Maroons Road
Winnipeg, Manitoba R3G OL5

Team Colors: Red and Blue
Year Founded: 1979
Arena: Winnipeg Arena
Seating Capacity: 15,250

BEFORE A National Hockey League franchise came to the city of Winnipeg, recreational hockey was played in the Junior and Senior Hockey Leagues. But in 1972, Ben Hatskin found these names too plain and ordinary and renamed them as the ''Jets'' Leagues.

The name was very popular with the people in Winnipeg. The name tied in with Chicago's Bobby Hull, known as the ''Golden Jet'' and with Elton John's hit song, Benny and the Jets.

When Winnipeg was granted a National Hockey League franchise in 1979, the team was named Winnipeg Jets after the name of the existing city leagues.

According to public relations director Ralph Carter, ''the team name of Jets has no distinct reasoning that ties in with the city of Winnipeg. There is no true document on the subject. The name was just popular with the fans.''

However, the team logo does have some background. The jet airplane symbolizes that the team is on the rise—perhaps to the Stanley Cup Championships.

HOW DID THE Clarence Campbell Conference get its name?

When the league was split into two groups, one conference was named after the National Hockey League President who served for 32 years. During his term, Campbell was known for setting high standards that helped professional hockey reach new levels of play.

Prince of Wales Conference

National Hockey League

Boston Bruins

Boston Bruins
150 Causeway Street
Boston, MA 02114

Team Colors: Brown and Yellow
Year Founded: 1924
Arena: Boston Garden
Seating Capacity: 14,451

WHEN CHARLES ADAMS founded a professional hockey team in Boston on November 1, 1924, he struggled with the usual task of any new owner—find the proper name for his new team.

When Adams could not find an appropriate name, he held a contest to aid him with the job of finding a name which would best suit his new hockey club. However, Adams had a few stipulations that needed to be followed in naming the team.

Adams wanted the team colors to be brown and yellow—to match the color of his business stores located in Boston. He wanted the name to be compatible with these colors.

He also demanded that the nickname suggest strength and power, which are good characteristics for a winning hockey team.

Keeping these two qualifications in mind, the name of Boston Bruins was suggested via the contest and announced as the official name of the club.

Bruin, which is another name for bear, easily matched the colors because of the fact that most bears are dark brown in color. Secondly, the bruin is a fierce and deadly animal, that will not back down from a fight—ideal for a hockey team mascot.

Buffalo Sabres

Buffalo Sabres
Memorial Auditorium
Buffalo, NY 14202

Team Colors: Blue, Gold, and White
Year Founded: 1970
Arena: Memorial Auditorium
Seating Capacity: 16,433

WHEN BUFFALO was awarded a National Hockey League team in 1970, one of the goals of the team's management was to select a name that would disassociate itself from the usual Buffalo team titles.

A contest was held by the club to choose a name for the team. Over 13,000 entries were submitted and there were suggestions mailed from as far away as Vancouver, Maine, and even one from Germany.

The selection committee was looking for a name with the following qualifications: a name not in use by any other professional sports team, a name that would be easily used in headlines, and one that would stray from the traditional names associated with buffaloes.

Although four people suggested Buffalo Sabres, Robert Sonnelitter was declared the winner via a drawing and received a pair of season tickets for his efforts.

The name of Sabres fit the specifications perfectly, according to team public relations director Chuck Burr. A press release from his office read, "A sabre is reknowned as a clean, sharp, decisive, and penetrating weapon on offense, as well as a strong parrying weapon on defense."

Other team names suggested were Bees, Mugwumps, Flying Zeppelins, Knoxen, Herd, Border Riders, and Comets.

Hartford Whalers

Hartford Whalers
One Civic Center Plaza
Hartford, CT 06103

Team Colors: Blue and Green
Year Founded: 1972—World Hockey Association
Arena: Hartford Civic Center
Seating Capacity: 14,510

THE HARTFORD WHALERS, Connecticut's National Hockey League team, actually chose their team name because of the state animal, the whale.

Prior to the start of the 1972 hockey season, Hartford was given a World Hockey Association franchise. Team officials chose Whalers as their nickname because of two defined reasons.

Whalers incorporates the letters of the World Hockey Association—WHA—and as a complete word, reflects a bit of New England history and tradition. The connection between Connecticut and whaling is a very important part of New England history.

The current team logo, which is a green "W" with a blue whale tail on top, was created in 1980 by Bill Barnes, the team's Vice President of Marketing and Public Relations; and Peter Good, a commercial designer in the Hartford area.

"We wanted to use the 'W,' of course," explained Barnes, "which was part of our two previous logos and develop the whale's tail, which is the strongest part of the animal.

"Bringing those two elements together formed a third element of the logo, a white 'H' for Hartford. By juggling these around awhile, that's what we came up with."

Many people don't recognize the "H" immediately, but it is a very important dimension because it symbolizes the change from New England Whalers to Hartford's team.

"I feel our logo is the most attractive in the league," comments Barnes, "and it will be ours for years to come."

Montreal Canadiens

Club de Hockey Canadien, Inc.
2313 Ste-Catherine Quest
Montreal, Que. H3H 1N2

Team Colors: Red, White, and Blue
Year Founded: 1909
Arena: Montreal Forum
Seating Capacity: 16,084

PROFESSIONAL HOCKEY first came to Montreal in 1909, when Ottawa sportsman J. Ambrose O'Brien first put his team on the ice and gave it the simple name of Club de Hockey Canadien.

Only one year later, the Club was sold to George Kennedy who renamed the team Club Athletique Canadien.

By the 1916-1917 season, however, Kennedy again changed the name—this time to the original name of Club de Hockey Canadien as the team was en route to their first Stanley Cup.

New Jersey Devils

New Jersey Devils
Byrne Meadowlands Arena
P. O. Box 504
East Rutherford, NJ 07073

Team Colors: Green and Red
Year Founded: 1982
Arena: Byrne Arena
Seating Capacity: 19,100

LIKE MANY other team names, the Devils nickname was created in a contest by local fans. In 1982, after John McMullen purchased the Colorado Rockies (formerly the Kansas City Scouts), New Jersey had a new hockey team known as the New Jersey Devils.

Out of more than 10,000 suggestions, the Devils' name was submitted by over 2,400 contestants. After the New Jersey Hockey Club officials narrowed the suggestions to 10 different names, fans were asked to vote for the one they preferred as the team's name. The Devils name was the easy winner.

As the legend states, the New Jersey Devil is said to have been a half-man, half-beast that stalked the Pine Barrens of South Jersey for 250 years. Another tale has it that the Devil was the 13th child born to Mother Leeds, who was jinxed by gypsies she discovered on her property in Estelville in Atlantic County, New Jersey.

Adapting to a new environment of promise and hope, the Devils gave up the blue, gold and red of their hapless Colorado predecessors for a combination of red, green, black and white. A green circle serves as the background for the crest of the emblem which features a white "N" with a stylized "J" which boasts a devil's horn at the top and a barbed tail at the bottom.

"The goal judge will probably be dressed in a big red suit and poke the goalie for his sins with a pitchfork," said the team's goalie when the team emblem was first unveiled. "On the ice, it's not bad to play like a devil sometimes—as long as you're an angel off the ice."

Other team name suggestions included the Blades, Meadowlanders, Americans, Meadowlarks, Colonials, Jaguars, Gulls, Lightnings, Coastals, Patriots and Generals.

New York Islanders

New York Islanders
Nassau Veterans' Memorial Coliseum
Uniondale, NY 11553

Team Colors: Blue and Orange
Year Founded: 1972
Arena: Nassau Veterans' Memorial Coliseum
Seating Capacity: 15,861

LONG ISLAND, New York, received its first professional sports franchise on June 6, 1972, when a National Hockey League club was granted to the island.

Eleven years earlier, a contest had been held to name the new National League baseball team which would later become the New York Mets. One of the runner-up suggestions at that time had been Islanders.

So when Uniondale was given a hockey team, the team became known as the New York Islanders—only natural for the first major sports franchise associated with Long Island.

New York Rangers

New York Rangers
Madison Square Garden
Four Pennsylvania Plaza
New York, NY 10001

Team Colors: Blue and Red
Year Founded: 1926
Arena: Madison Square Garden
Seating Capacity: 17,500

IN 1926, seeing the great popularity of the New York Americans of the National Hockey League, Madison Square Garden President Tex Rickard decided to acquire a team under direct ownership of the Garden.

With the Western Hockey League nearing bankruptcy, Rickard found this was the perfect time to acquire high caliber players. In addition to the New York club, the Detroit Cougars and Chicago Black Hawks entered the NHL in 1926.

The Rangers team name was named for President Rickard and the unofficial team name of "Tex's Rangers."

Philadelphia Flyers

Philadelphia Flyers
The Spectrum
Philadelphia, PA 19148-5290

Team Colors: Orange, Black, and White
Year Founded: 1967
Arena: The Spectrum
Seating Capacity: 17,077

WHEN THE National Hockey League selected its first expansion team in 1967, the new franchise was given to Ed Snider of Philadelphia.

Immediately following Philadelphia's acceptance to the NHL, general manager Bud Poile and the board of directors organized a public contest to name the team. Out of 25,000 entries the committee chose Philadelphia Flyers as the new team name—mainly because it sounded proper after the word Philadelphia.

After the team nickname was chosen, the Flyers went to Mel Richman's advertising agency to develop a team logo and trademark. The franchise is portrayed through the stylized "P" with wings, which symbolizes the city of Philadelphia and the wings denote the Flyers' name.

Pittsburgh Penguins

Pittsburgh Penguins
Gate 7 - Civic Arena
Pittsburgh, PA 15219

Team Colors: Black, Gold, and White
Year Founded: 1967
Arena: Pittsburgh Civic Arena
Seating Capacity: 16,033

UNLIKE MOST other professional sports nicknames, the Pittsburgh Penguins of the National Hockey League has a nickname that has no tie in with its home town.

In 1967, when Pittsburgh was granted an NHL franchise, team officials decided to host a public contest to name their new hockey club. After looking at all the suggestions, the name of Pittsburgh Penguins was announced as the official team name.

"The Penguin name is not symbolic of any part of Pittsburgh as the Steelers are of the NFL," said public relations assistant Cindy Heine. "There is no direct reasoning behind the name. It was just chosen as a nickname."

Quebec Nordiques

Le Club de Hockey Les Nordiques
2205 Ave du Colisee
Quebec, Que. G1L 4W7

Team Colors: Red, White, and Blue
Year Founded: 1972—World Hockey Association
Arena: The Quebec Coliseum
Seating Capacity: 15,434

THE DECISION for a new professional hockey team in the city of Quebec began in 1971, when six businessmen sold the Quebec Remparts and then began their search for a new team in which to reinvest.

On February 11, 1972, the search was over. Jean-Marc Bruneau along with associates Marius Fortier and John Dacres purchased the rights to the San Francisco franchise in the new-born World Hockey Association and moved the team to Quebec.

On May 5 of the same year, the team name of Quebec Nordiques was announced. The jury that made the selection stated that the reasoning behind the name was that the Quebec team was now the most Northern team in professional hockey.

After much success in the WHA, National Hockey League President John Ziegler announced the admittance of the Nordiques to the NHL along with three other WHA teams on March 30, 1979. Although the team began play in a new league, it continued under the same Nordique name.

THE PRINCE OF WALES Conference is named after the Prince of Wales Trophy. The Prince of Wales sponsored a trophy for the winner of the Montreal Canadiens/New York Rangers game on December 15, 1925.

The sterling silver trophy, with the Prince's Coat of Arms engraved on it, cost $2,500 in 1925. It is presented each year to the team who wins the league title and is second in prominence only to the Stanley cup.

Washington Capitals

Washington Capitals
Landover, MD 20785

WASHINGTON
capit**als**®

Team Colors: Red, White, and Blue
Year Founded: 1973
Arena: Capital Centre
Seating Capacity: 18,130

WHEN THE National Hockey League awarded the District of Columbia a franchise in 1973, it was assumed that the new club's name would somehow be associated with the nation's capital.

The team uniform was designed by team owner Abe Pollin, general manager Milt Schmidt, Wilson Sporting Goods, and Fred Reithlingshoefer—an independent artist. They selected the team colors of red, white and blue—which were taken from the United States flag, which is always seen high in the sky throughout the city.

A contest was held to determine a team nickname. Washington Capitals was selected as the winner, named after the nation's capital located in the heart of Washington, D. C.